Forgiveness Is Not as Hard as You Make It

Nathan Frazier

ISBN 978-1-0980-0279-4 (paperback)
ISBN 978-1-0980-0280-0 (digital)

Christian Faith Publishing, Inc.
832 Park Avenue
Meadville, PA 16335
www.christianfaithpublishing.com

Printed in the United States of America

Chapter 1

I t was mid-Saturday afternoon, there were six guys who were best friends, playing a game of basketball. It was a hot day with a light breeze blowing across the court.

They had been best friends since childhood and they loved to play ball every Saturday. However, this particular Saturday, the more they played, the more intense the game got. They always played on the same team for a few months, and then they would switch up.

The game had gotten heated, and the guys began to get very physical to the point of causing physical harm. They weren't angry with each other, but it seemed as though they had a score to settle. They were doing a lot of trash talk between them. If you didn't know them, you would wonder if they were really best friends. They were pushing, shoving, and elbowing each other. These guys loved sports and they loved to compete. But most of all they loved each other. It didn't matter if they were playing the game or watching it on television, they were truly sports fanatics. Their names were Jackie, Tyrone, Mark, Tyler, Conner, Danny, and Michael.

Tyler and Conner were white and the other four were black. Tyler and Conner were roommates and they lived across town. When they played ball, they were on opposing teams. These guys were playing an aggressive game.

Conner was on Tyrone's team. They all looked up to Tyrone for one reason: he was the oldest and the wisest of the group. The game was tied. Conner had the ball and Tyler was guarding him. Conner jumped up to make a pass to Tyrone. But when he went up and released the ball, Tyler tried to block his pass, but he missed, and when he came down, Tyler elbowed Conner in the chest on his collar bone. When Tyrone received the ball, he drove in hard to dunk the ball. When he did this, he smashed the goal so hard, he bent the rim. That was the winning point of the game.

All the fellows on Tyrone's team were bragging about the game, and celebrating their win. Conner noticed that he wasn't feeling too good in his chest. But he kept on celebrating his team win. He thought that he might be feeling this way because of the physical contact of the game.

After all of the celebration and bragging, Conner and Tyler went back to their apartment. On the way back, Conner was bragging to Tyler about their winning. Tyler didn't like it, and he was getting irritated because of the lost. That was the third time that Tyler's team had loss to Conner's team.

When they arrived at the apartment, Conner sat in a chair and started to feel worse. He got up and went to the bathroom to take a shower. When he took his shirt off, he noticed a bruise and a little swelling on his chest under his collar bone. After he took his shower, he was in great pain. The pain was getting worse, and then he became short of breath, which worried him.

Tyler was in the room, anticipating the basketball game that was about to start. Conner called out to Tyler to take him to the hospital, and that he needed to go now. But to Conner's surprise, Tyler told him that he couldn't do it right then. The game was about to start. Tyler was still irritated about losing the game again. Tyler had never treated Conner this way before. This was out of character for Tyler. The game was the final of the playoff. Tyler had a small bet on this game. He didn't want to miss it.

Conner said to him, "Man, I need to go, I am feeling bad."

Tyler said, "Man, why do you have to go; now? The game is coming on. Let me see. It ain't that bad, you'll be all right. You're just bruised because we played hard."

Conner pleaded with him. Conner said, "Man, I don't want to die, I don't want to die."

"Man, you ain't gone die," Tyler said.

"I need to go to the hospital. Man, please don't let me die." He cried out, "I feel real bad. I don't want to die." Conner was very weak, and he saw that Tyler was not going to take him to the hospital. The hospital was only a few blocks down the street; he felt like he could walk it. He used what energy he had to get out of that apartment to seek help. As he made his way out on to the streets, he felt weaker. There was a van with three black men in it. They had stopped because traffic was backed up.

These three guys were on their way to their men's Bible study class that they have every other Saturday evening. Conner leaned in on the side of the van, on the passenger door, and asked them if they would take him to the hospital. He told them that he was very sick. They looked at each other, and with hesitation, they agreed to help the young man. They started to tell him no, but something deep down inside told them to say yes.

They loaded him into the van, and on the way to the hospital, two of the guys noticed that Conner was not looking to good at all. As a matter of fact, he was very pale and changing colors. He looked worse once he was in the van. He looked like he had been beaten. His neck and the chin were turning black and blue. Now they began to panic on the way to the hospital.

They were very scared. They started to question themselves on why they picked this guy up. "If he dies in this van, it will look like we did this to him."

Chapter 2

These three guys used to make their living hustling in the streets. They never committed any violent crime, but they had been in and out of jail. They were getting tired of the same old game. They felt like that there had to be something better.

Someone had talked to them about turning their lives around and giving their lives to God. It took a while to think about it. They decided one day to make a change and give their lives to the Lord. They started going to church more and more. Every Sunday in the pastor's message, he would tell the congregation that they must repent of their sins. One Sunday, the three friends went to the altar to repent and they asked God to forgive them of their sins.

They were smart young men, and they knew that this transition was a new way of life, and they were going to stick with it. They knew that if they continued on the path that they were on, their lives may be cut short, so the guys gave up the street life. They started to participate in the church activities, and the more they did, the more they enjoyed doing so. Their names are Jackie, Sam, and Kenneth.

They basically grew up together in the same neighborhood. The neighborhood they grew up in was not a very good neighborhood. There were a lot of drugs, gang violence, and shootings going on. It wasn't a good place to raise children, but they survived. They grew up poor, but they were happy. They were always good kids with kind hearts, but they always stayed in trouble. They knew how to survive in the streets, and they always had each other's back.

Now they had made a commitment to be disciples for God. One thing about these friends, once they made a commitment, they put their hearts into it. They knew that the new road that they were traveling now was not going to be easy. They learned that from the Bible classes that they had been having. But they were determined to stay committed to God and make a better life for themselves. As long as they stayed friends, they were a support system to each other. They found jobs with decent pay, and they made the best of what they had until they could do better. At least they weren't hustling in the streets and always looking back over their shoulders.

Chapter 3

"What will people say if this guy dies in our van?" Kenneth asked the question. "They will say we killed this guy, and we don't even know who he is."

They called on God and asked God to help this young man and not let him die. They were praying hard. They started to get scared. Traffic was slow, but it was steady moving. It seemed as if Conner was not going to make it to the hospital alive.

Conner, with a weak voice, kept repeating, "Please don't let me die."

Jackie said, "Hang in there, buddy, we are almost there." Sam and Jackie were sweating profusely.

They made it to the hospital and dropped him off in the emergency room. Conner was in and out of consciousness and was unable to tell the doctors what happened to him.

The doctor turned and asked, "What's your name?"

Jackie replied, "My name is Jackie."

The doctor asked, "What happened to him? Do you know his name?"

Jackie told the doctor that he didn't know what happened to him, and no, he didn't know his name. "He just walked up to the van and asked us to help him get to the hospital and so we did." Jackie was looking nervous and sweat was steady dripping down his face.

The doctor looked as if he didn't believe him. The doctor said, "Okay, just stay right here. I'll be right back."

The nurse took the patient's shirt off to examine him and noticed that his chest, his abdomen, and up around his neck was black and blue and swollen. He looked as if he had been beaten. The doctor ordered a CAT scan of his chest and abdomen. When the results came back, they showed that he had internal bleeding going on. They rushed him to surgery. The ER doctor called the surgeon in for emergency surgery. In the meantime, he returned to the waiting area to talk to the three young men that brought the patient in, only to find that they had left.

Conner was in surgery for three hours. He made it through surgery, but he was in critical condition and he had lost a lot of blood. He was placed in an induced coma and put on a ventilator in ICU. The doctor was not sure if he was going to pull through. The hospital admitted him under the name John Doe 459.

Chapter 4

In the meantime, the hospital staff notified the police and reported that three black men brought a white male into the emergency room, who appeared to have been beaten near death, but that they were long gone. They didn't stick around to answer any questions. They looked very suspicious. The police asked if they could describe the vehicle that they were driving and a description of the men. The staff began to stereotype the young men. One of the nurses told the police that one of the guys had a tattoo on his hands that looked like he was in a gang and a small scar near his right eye. Another had long hair like dreadlocks. The one that the doctor spoke with said his name was Jackie. He acted like he was the leader. They acted very nervous and suspicious.

Jackie, Kenneth, and Sam had gone on to their men's Bible study class. They left the hospital because they were running late.

Kenneth said, "Man, I hope that he will be all right." They arrived at the church and started their class. The pastor was teaching out of the book of Acts chapter 12. This is when Peter was bound and locked up in jail to be killed, but the church was praying for him, and miraculously, he escaped from prison. The pastor also talked about how Paul and Silas were put in prison. But while they were there, at midnight, they prayed and sang hymns. They didn't worry, because they knew that what they were doing was for God, and He had their backs.

These three friends had no idea what they were about to face because of their act of kindness. The new life that they were living brought them great joy. They had good jobs and they were in good relationships and they had new friends in the church. Life seemed to be too good to be true.

After Bible study was over, they spoke with the pastor and told him what had happened earlier that day. The pastor commended them on the good deed that they did by helping another brother in need, regardless who he was.

When they left Bible study, they were still concerned about the guy that they had taken to the ER. They were hoping that he made it there in time. They went home to get ready for church the next day. They shared a three-bedroom apartment together.

Sunday morning, they got up. They were feeling pretty good. They were ready for a great service at church.

"Man, I have a good feeling that the Lord is going to be in a blessing business today," said Sam. They made it to church, and sure enough, there was a whole lot of praising going on. During church service, the spirit of the Lord had filled the building. People were rejoicing all over the place. They were falling out because they were overcome by the Holy Spirit. People were shouting, singing, dancing, and running all over the building, crying and praising God.

The pastor was feeling full of the Holy Spirit as he brought the word of God. As he was preaching, the congregation could not sit still. This was an unusual Sunday; everybody was shouting, *"Amen Amen!"* They were full of the Holy Spirit, and they didn't want the services to end.

After church service, the three fellows went out to dinner with their lady friends and had fellowship with each other as they normally do. Their conversation was about the pastor's sermon and how they were filled with the Holy Spirit. His sermon topic was to never let go of your faith. He came from the book of Hebrews 11:6,

> But without faith it is impossible to please Him,
> for he who comes to God must believe that He
> is, and that He reward those who diligently seek
> Him.

Jackie said he felt like the pastor was talking directly to him. Kenneth and Sam said they felt the same thing.

"Do you think that God is trying to tell us something?" Sam asked.

Kenneth and Jackie said at the same time, "I don't know."

They knew that deep in their hearts that they are saved by the Holy Spirit. They agreed to go by the hospital on Tuesday after work to see if the young man had made it.

Chapter 5

Tyler had fallen asleep during the game. He got up mid-Sunday morning unaware of what was going on. He started making breakfast. Suddenly, he remembered his friend was not feeling very well the day before. He felt bad about the way he treated his best friend. So he started looking for Conner so that he could apologize to him, but he couldn't find him. He went to Conner's room door and knocked, but there was no answer.

Well, maybe he is asleep, Tyler thought. He knocked again, but this time a little harder. The door pushed open just a little, and Tyler peeped in, but he could not see his bed. Then he opened the door wider. He noticed that Conner had not slept in his bed all night, and he began to get worried

"Where is Conner? What happened to him? Maybe one of the guys came over and took him to the hospital. I'll call Danny to see if he knows anything. Hello, hey, Danny, how are you?"

Danny replied, "Okay, what's up?"

"Hey, man, have you heard from or seen Conner?"

"No! What's going on?" he asked.

"Well, yesterday he said that he wasn't feeling so well. I went and watched the game and fell asleep, I just woke up. Tyler wasn't telling the whole truth. I looked for him in his room this morning, but he's not here."

"No, I haven't seen him. Have you called the other fellows?" said Danny.

Tyler replied, "I will check around." Tyler called everyone he knew, but he had no luck in finding Conner. He was panicking and worried. "Where could Conner be? I'll call the hospital."

"Rock Hill General Hospital, how may I assist you?"

"My name is Tyler, and I'm looking for a friend that might be a patient there. His name is Conner Edenfield, he may have come in on Saturday night."

"Okay, let me see," said the operator. "I'm sorry sir, but I don't have anyone by that name."

Tyler was about to lose his mind. He was full of guilt. "If anything happened to him, how can I forgive myself for not being there for him? Oh my goodness, what am I going to do? I need to call the police. If he is missing, they are going to blame me. Oh! Man, I need to call his father. He will be mad at me and blame me too. Oh! God, what am I to do? Okay, get yourself together," he said to himself. "I have to call the police to report that he is missing. Oh man! Conner, where are you?"

"Hello, Rock Hill Police Department."

"Hi, my name is Tyler Monroe and my friend is missing and I can't find him."

"Hold on a minute and let me connect you to the missing persons department."

"Missing persons, can I help you?"

"Yes sir. My name is Tyler and I can't find my friend."

"What's your last name Tyler?"

"Monroe."

"Okay, Mr. Monroe. What is your friend's name?"

"Conner."

"How long has your friend been missing?"

"When I got up this morning, he wasn't in his room," said Tyler.

The officer said to Tyler, "Look, your friend has to be missing for forty-eight hours before we can do anything. He may have stayed with a friend or something. Call us back when it has been forty-eight hours."

"But he was sick," said Tyler.

The officer said, "We still can't do anything until the forty-eight hours are up."

After Tyler got off the phone, he was upset even more. *Maybe he did go to his parents' house. But if he is not there, then I would have to explain to them what happened to their son. He is going to be pissed and blame me. But whatever it is, I have to let them know that their son is missing.*

"Hello!"

"Hi, Mr. Edenfield. This is Tyler. How are you, sir?"

"Oh! Tyler, hi, I'm doing fine." He was saying this as if he was happy to hear from Tyler. "And how are you?"

"I'm well, sir. Hey, Mr. Edenfield, I'm looking for Conner. Is he over there?"

"No. I haven't seen him. Is everything okay?"

"Well, sir, I haven't seen Conner all day, and I haven't heard from him. I am concerned."

"What do you mean that you haven't heard nor seen him all day?" Mr. Edenfield responded with a stern voice. Now Mr. Edenfield was getting worried. It was not like Conner to take off and not let someone know where he is. "Have you been out looking for him? Have you called the police? Have you called your friends?"

"Yes, sir, I've done all that. That's why I'm calling you. I don't know what else to do."

"I'm on my way over there. I don't want to tell his mother until we know for sure what is going on."

Chapter 6

The next morning, Jackie, Kenneth, and Sam went to their jobs as usual. When Jackie got up that morning, he said his prayers, but he had a funny feeling come over him, and he didn't know why. It was like a sick feeling in his stomach—it wasn't a pain but a queasy feeling. He went on to work anyway.

The media had received word that an unidentified young man was admitted to the hospital over the weekend, who was badly beaten and near death.

"The police are looking for three men for questioning. They know that one went by the name of Jackie. If anybody has any information, please call the police."

Now the pastor had the television on when he heard the news report. He was wondering if the Jackie that he knew was the same one that the media was talking about. He sent Jackie a text for the three of them to meet him at the church after they get off work.

The pastor remembered the good deed that they told him over the weekend. The pastor knew the history of the three young men. He knew that they had been in trouble with the law before. He also had seen the change and the progress that they have made. He couldn't help but to think, *Have they truly made a change their lives? Are they pretending to be followers of Christ and still living the street life? Were they really telling me the truth about what really happened?*

The pastor was starting to have doubt, but he was going to trust them and believe in them. He also knew how the devil would play mind tricks, how he put doubt in one's spirit. He was not going to let the devil use him to doubt what these young men were going to say.

Jackie had texted Sam and Kenneth early in the day to come by the church when they got off. When they arrived, they met with the pastor in his study.

"What's going on pastor?" Jackie asked.

The pastor said, "Tell me what happened with that fellow you took to the hospital on Saturday. Tell me what really happened."

"Why? What's going on? Did he die?"

"I need you to tell me what really happened so that I can help you."

Kenneth spoke up and said, "Help *us*! Help us with *what*? Nothing happened. This guy came up to the van and asked us to help him get to the hospital. He looked real sick. We took him there and left. What is this all about anyway?"

The pastor asked if they had seen the news today. Sam said no, he didn't.

Kenneth said, "We've been working all day. What's going on pastor? Will you get to the point?" Nervousness and fear were overcoming the three of them.

"The news is reporting that a young man was taken to the hospital this weekend and was badly beaten. He is in critical condition. The police are looking for three black men, and they have the first name of one the guys."

"And who is that?" Jackie asked.

"It's your name, Jackie."

"My name! We didn't beat nobody. We helped that guy. Why would we jump on somebody for no reason?" Jackie spoke out in anger.

The pastor spoke up, "Calm down. I believe you. We will work this out."

"We came to you and told you what happened, and you're acting like you don't believe us," said Kenneth.

"I believe you."

Sam asked, "What is there to work out?"

"Let us call the police so that you can tell your side of the story, so that this can get cleared up," the pastor said.

Jackie said with anger and a loud voice, "Our side of the story—there is no story! There is only the truth!"

The pastor said, "I know that you are angry and that is understandable but—"

Sam cut him off: "We're all angry!"

The pastor went on to say, "We have to call the police tonight so that they can get to the bottom of this matter."

"Okay, call them!" Jackie said. "Here we are trying to do the right thing and getting blamed for someone else's wrong. Is God punishing us for something we did?"

"No, son, don't blame God. He will work it out for you," said the pastor.

"We are trying to do all that God required us to do. So why are we being blamed for this? Why is God allowing this to happen to us?" Jackie said.

"We can't talk nor think like that," Kenneth said. "We have been through a lot of tough times together, and we survived; we can make it through this. We have to stand with each other and keep the faith."

Jackie and Sam agreed with Kenneth. The pastor called the police.

Chapter 7

"Code blue ICU, code blue ICU, code blue ICU."

The nurses and doctors rush into the patient's room. Alarms were going off. The patient's nurse had already started CPR.

The doctor asked, "How long have you been doing CPR?" His nurse said it's been about 2 minutes since she started CPR. She said she walked in to give him his meds, and he started to go into arrest.

"What have you given him?"

"Nothing yet. He just coded."

The doctor said, "Continue CPR and give him one round of epi. Stand by to shock. Stop CPR. Okay, shock!"

"Clear, all clear!"

"Shock!" The doctor looked at monitor—no change. "Continue CPR."

"Restarting CPR," the nurse said.

"Has it been three minutes yet?" Another nurse shouted yes. "Okay, give him another round of epi and continue CPR. Four minutes has past. Okay, stop CPR and check for a pulse."

"No pulse."

"Start CPR and give Amiodarone. Has it been three minutes yet?"

"Yes," the nurse said.

"Stop CPR and check for a pulse."

Nurse said, "Nothing happening, and he is not looking good."

The doctor said, "I know, continue CPR."

The nurse called out to the doctor, "Doctor, it's been one hour and fifteen minutes. I guess we are going to have to call it."

"Stop CPR and check the pulse."

As the nurse checked the pulse, the room was very quiet and filled with sadness. The only sound was a steady *beeeep*. The rhythm on the monitor was Asystole. No heartbeat.

The doctor said, "We'll call it. The time is 8:30 p.m." They all walked out of the room very sad. Two nurses started to cry, and three other nurses tried to comfort them. They were new nurses and had never experienced a situation like this before.

Chapter 8

The police arrived at the church, and the pastor met them at the door.

"Hi, my name is detective Garrison, and these are my partners Detective Patterson, Officer Raymond, and Officer Daniels. I spoke to you on the phone and you stated that the three suspects that we are looking for are with you. May we have a word with them?"

"Yeah sure, officer. They are in my study. Follow me," the pastor replied.

As the police met with Jackie, Kenneth and Sam, Officer Garrison introduced himself and the other officers with him.

Officer Garrison started asking the three young men questions about the young man that they took to the hospital on Saturday evening. "Did you know him?"

All three shook their heads and answered no.

"How did you all come to meet the young man?"

Jackie answered, "Like I told the doctor at the hospital, we were stopped in traffic, and he came up to the van that we were in and asked if we could take him to the hospital. He looked very weak and sick. We were on our way to Bible study, and we were going in that direction anyway. So we agreed to drop him off. He kept asking us to please not let him die. Kenneth told him to hang in there and that we were almost there. He was alive when we got him to the hospital. So we left and went on to Bible study. We didn't know him, so we left him at the hospital. And that's it."

Detective Garrison didn't believe them. "We need to take you all to the station for further questioning and to get an official statement."

Sam asked, "Are we under arrest?"

"No, we just have to ask a few more questions, and we need to get a full statement."

They arrived at the police station, and the police separated the three young men and placed them in a room by themselves. They were questioned by different officers, they gave the same answer.

Detective Garrison entered the room that Jackie was in and started telling Jackie about the condition of the man that they took to the hospital. "The doctors said that the young man you brought to the hospital was severely beaten, and I just received word that he died a couple hours ago. So I'm placing you and your friends under arrest for the death of that young man."

"How can you arrest us, and you don't have a name of the person?"

"We don't have his name yet, but we are working on finding out who he is."

"We did not kill anybody. We tried to help him!" shouted Jackie.

"You have been in and out of jail since you were a juvenile!" said Detective Garrison in a high-pitched voice. Detective Garrison was angry because he thought that these black young men killed a white young man for no reason. He was making this personal. He asked, "Why should we believe you now?"

"We may have been in and out of jail, but we have never caused harm and, least to say, killed anyone," Jackie said.

Detective Garrison said, "The evidence points to you. Officer, take them in the back to be processed."

Jackie said, "This is not right. We have done nothing wrong. What evidence do you have to hold us? I need to make a phone call."

Detective Garrison told the officer to let him make the call and then process them. "By the way you and your friends were the last to talk to him. As far as we know, you could have taken him to the hospital so you could have an alibi."

Jackie made the call to the pastor. "Hello, hello, pastor, we need your help. They are booking us for the death of the man that we were trying to help. They said he died a few hours ago. We didn't do it. Can you get us out of here? We are innocent! Can you bail us out?"

"Oh my God!" The pastor replied. "I'm sorry, but there is nothing that I can do for the three of you tonight. It may take a couple of days, but I will work on it. I need to make some calls. In the meantime, keep your head up and don't lose faith. I know that you all are innocent, and I know that God will work it out to your good."

"Pastor, I know he will," Jackie said. "But why did he allow this to happen to us?"

The pastor said, "I don't know why God has chosen the three of you. But for whatever the reason, it is for His glory. I know that this is easy for me to say because I'm not in your shoes. I want the three of you to use this time to pray and meditate on the goodness of God. Remember what Paul and Silas did when they were in prison. Don't lose your faith, and He will reveal His plan to you. I will do whatever I can do to get you all out. You are some fine young men, and you have a lot of support from the church."

Jackie hung up the phone, and the officer took him to the back where his two friends were already locked up and placed them in a cell together. When Jackie was pushed into the cell, Sam and Kenneth rushed to assist him. They asked him, "What in the world is going on?"

Jackie said, "Man, the guy that we took to the hospital, they are saying that we beat him and now he is dead. Now we are being charged for his death."

Kenneth said, "Man, this is crazy! You know we didn't do that, and they know it! Man, why God is doing this to us? Here we are back in jail, we may lose our jobs and our home and our friends. How is the church going to look at us now? It looks like we can never get a break."

Jackie spoke up and said, "Man, I talked to the pastor, and he is going help us to get out of here. But it's going to take some time."

Sam spoke up and said, "Looks like all we have is time. It doesn't look like we're going anywhere."

Jackie said, "The pastor told me that we should take this time to reflect on the goodness of God, pray and to meditate."

"How can we meditate when we are being charged with murder?" Sam asked, "Man, God is punishing us for what we did when we were younger."

Jackie responded, "Man, what is wrong with you? As long as things were going well for you, you trust and believe in Him. But now that a little storm has come up in your life, you want to throw in the towel and quit. You want to give up on God. Where is your faith? This is what the devil wants us to do—to give up on God. So all that negative talk, we can't do. We have to trust in the Lord. I didn't turn my life over to Him for nothing. When we committed, we knew the road was going to be rough. I believe that this is a test of our faith. We have been friends for a very long time. We have been in situations that none of us knew how we were going to get out of. But somehow, we did."

Sam said, "Yeah, man, you're right. I know how we got out of them. God brought us out."

Jackie said, "Yes, he did. And look at this: during that time, we were not saved. But still, He worked it out for us. Now that we are saved by His blood, I must believe—I have to believe—that He will work this out for us. I also believe that we will come out better than we came in. If we lose our jobs, He gave it to us. If we lose our apartment, He gave it to us. We can lose all that we have as long as we don't lose hope. Like I said, this is just a test, and I intend to pass it. It is up to us to hold each other up. If one falls, the other two must pick the fallen one up. So let's hold each other up.

"There are so many people who say that they love God and that they trust Him, but as soon as they are faced with trouble, they lose hope and they lose faith. We will not be like that. We will not give into fear. We are going to fight this fight. When I read the book of Daniel about the three Hebrew boys and how they stood their ground with what they believed in, I must stay encouraged. They didn't lose faith even though they were faced with losing their lives. They knew that God was going to deliver them, and if He didn't, they knew that He was able. That's the kind of faith that I have."

As Jackie was speaking, two young men in the cell next to them were listening with full attention. One of them spoke up and said, "I'm sorry for standing here listing to your conversation, but what you were saying got my attention. I have heard people talk about this God that you're talking about but never like the way you talk about Him. What is being saved all about? I've never been to church. You speak with so much excitement. Tell me about being saved and how can I get saved?"

The other young man said, "Me too. Because I want something different. There has to be a better life than this."

Jackie said, "Brother, don't be sorry. For we were in your shoes at one point in our lives, and someone introduced us to Jesus. Yes, to your statement, there is a better life than what you are living."

The young man told Jackie that he wanted to be saved and ask if he could save him. Jackie responded, "I have no authority to save anybody. Only Jesus has the authority and only Jesus can save your soul."

The young man said, "I have done a lot of wrong in my life. With all that I've done, your God wants to save me. People always judged me and looked down on me. Do you think that He will save a sinner like me?"

Jackie said, "I am not one to judge, and Jesus didn't come to condemn the world, but to save it. In order to be saved, you must believe in the Lord Jesus Christ. In Romans 10:8–9, it says, 'The Word is near you, in your mouth and in your heart [that is the word of faith which we preach], that if you confess with your mouth the Lord Jesus and believe in your heart that God has raised Him from the dead, you will be saved.'"

The two young men confessed in that hour, and they were saved. Now Jackie, Sam, and Kenneth started to rejoice and praised God for His saving grace. They started singing. Other fellows in the jail joined in on the praising and worshipping. This went on through the night.

Before the night was over, six people had confessed their sins and given their lives to the Lord.

Chapter 9

There was one fellow who started singing. His voice was so amazing and smooth. When he started to sing, everyone else got very quiet. His voice was carried all over the building. There was a stillness in the building. His jail cell was across from Kenneth's cell.

When he was done singing, Kenneth asked him, "What church do you attend?"

He said, "I don't."

"Why not?" Kenneth asked.

The young man responded and said, "I messed up and was looked down on by the people in the church that I attended. They showed no love. They say they love everybody, but they didn't show it. I messed up. They talked about me behind my back. I embarrassed my family. Some had their cliques, so I stopped going, and I haven't been back to a church since. I used to be a choir director."

"I hear you, my friend, and I can hear the hurt in your song. When I was listening to you sing, I could hear the longing to be close to God. There is a battle going on inside of you, and you don't want to acknowledge that God is calling on you to come back to Him.

"In the Bible, Paul tells us that we shouldn't let nothing separate us from the love of God which is in Christ Jesus our Lord. We worry about what other people do and what they say. You can't control what other people say and do. You can only control what you say and do and how you react. You pass judgement on all churches based on your experience with one church that you felt mistreated you. What you have done was to try to justify your reason to not worship God.

You are trying to make this all about you. It is not about you, it's about the love of Jesus Christ and the love that you should have for others.

"Jesus tells us that in order to be one of His disciples, we must deny ourselves. No matter what you have done or how dirty you may think you are, Jesus can wash you as white as snow. Open the window of your heart and let the light of Jesus shine through. God gave you a gift to reach His people, the ones who are saved and the ones who are not saved. All that you have been through, God allowed it to be. He has been molding you and shaping you into that man—that *strong* man that He wants you to be. He has a plan for you and He will see it through. I can't tell you what to do with your life, but what I can do is encourage you to let go of your anger, your fears, your bitterness, and allow God to work through you so that He can get the glory."

The young man said, "I hear what you're saying. And you are right. When I get out, I will seek another church."

Kenneth asked him, "What is your name?" He said his name was Kelvin. "Well, Kelvin, I would like to exchange numbers with you so that we could stay in touch with each other."

"I'm not sure about that," Kelvin said.

"Why not?" Kenneth asked. "What are you really afraid of?"

Kelvin said, "I'm not afraid. I just don't trust people to do what they say they're going to do. Like I said, I have been disappointed too many times by Christian folks."

Kenneth said, "Can I ask you a question?"

Kelvin said, "Yes, ask away."

"If you have two friends whom you really care about, but one friend turned his back on you and hurt your feelings. Do you dislike both friends because of what one friend did?"

Kelvin said, "No, only the one who turned on me."

"Then why do you turn away from Christians who cause you no harm? Why do you blame all churches for something that one church did?"

Kelvin set back on his bunkbed and began to dwell on what Kenneth had said.

Kenneth said to Kelvin, "You know, some Christians always blame someone else for their failures when it is their own fault. No one is in control of you but you."

Sam, Kenneth, and Jackie were giving God His glory all night long. They had forgotten what they were in jail for. By morning, they were so tired, the only thing that they could do was to sleep. Before they laid down to sleep, they looked at each other.

Jackie said, "Can you believe what happened last night?"

Sam said, "Man, if I wasn't here to witness it, it would be hard to believe. Jackie, I realize now why we are here. This is what God wanted us to do—to be a witness to lost souls. I am definitely sure that God will deliver us from this bondage. I'm not worried."

Kenneth said, "Thank you, Jackie, for that talk last night. You help me keep my head straight."

After being up all night they laid down to get some sleep.

Chapter 10

The next morning, Nurse Mary had returned to work from a long-weekend vacation retreat. It was a vacation that was well needed. She had been under a lot of stress and had also been working a lot of overtime because the hospital were understaff. The overtime and the stress were getting the best of her.

A church in the community had sponsored a women's retreat. The retreat allowed the women to come together under a sisterhood. She used her vacation time so that she could arrive two days early to relax and sight-see before the convention started. There were about three hundred women that came together to bond, relax, to make a connection, and get closer to God. It was a chance to renew their sprit, mind, body, and soul. They had renowned speakers to motivate, to encourage, and to renew their hope. It was an uplifting weekend, and no one wanted it to end. But they had to return to work.

She arrived to work happy. Her coworkers could see the joy on her face and in her steps, and she looked refreshed.

One coworker said to her, "Look at you, that weekend getaway did you a lot of good. I haven't seen you this happy in a long time."

Mary said, "Girl, you just don't know. That was the best thing that I could have ever done. I can't wait until next year to go again. We had a blast! I want to tell you all about it, but we will have to talk later because if I start talking about it now, I won't stop talking."

At the change of shifts, Mary was told by the in-charge nurse that they had eight patients on the floor, and there were four nurses today, so they have two patients each to care for. "There may be another nurse coming up to help later this morning. All the patients are stable and doing well. We had two John Does that came in over the weekend. You wouldn't believe how the weekend went. One didn't make it. The other one is stable, and he looks like he is going to make a full recovery. Mary, you will be caring for patients in room 457 and 458. Kathy will be caring for room 459 and 460. Tina, you will care for 455 and 456. Terry you are assigned to rooms 450 and 451. Is everybody good? Are there any questions? Okay, let's get started."

All the nurses went to their assigned patient's rooms to introduce themselves and assess their patients. Mary talked with her patients to find out if they needed anything and made sure that they were comfortable. Her patients were stable and were not on a vent. She checked in on them every fifteen minutes.

One of Kathy's patients was on a vent, and he was the John Doe. She had to change his bandages, but she needed some help. She asked Mary if she had few minutes, and if so, could she help her change his bandages.

Mary said, "Sure, but let me check on my patients first."

As she was helping Kathy, she thought she might know the patient. But she was not sure. She kept helping Kathy with the bandages, and at the same time, she kept saying, "I think I know this guy."

Kathy asked, "How do you know him?"

Mary said, "I'm not sure."

After they were done with the bandages, Mary went back to her station and started monitoring her patients. While she was monitoring her patients, all she could think about was the patient that she think she though she knew.

Two hours later, she peeped into Kathy patient's room to take another look at the patient and said, "Oh my God! That is my brother's best friend. His name is Conner. He is the mayor's son. Tyron told me that he was missing and they have been looking for him. Oh my God!" Mary said, "Has anybody been up here or called?"

Kathy said, "No one." Kathy asked, "Are you sure he is who you say he is?"

Mary said, "Yes, I'm sure. I am very sure."

Kathy said, "We have to notify the supervisor so that someone can notify the next of kin. I know his family is worried."

The supervisor of the hospital called the mayor's office, but he was not in. The receptionist told her that he was in a meeting at the police station with the chief of police. "Maybe if you call over there, you can reach him."

Chapter 11

The mayor had wanted to meet with the chief of police in his office to talk about the violence in the city. He wanted to talk about a plan of action that could be done to curve the violence that was plaguing the city. The city crime rate had gone up about 6 percent in the last year. The city and county jail were already overcrowded. The majority of the people in jail were not violent people. They were put in jail for misdemeanor charges.

As the mayor was talking to the chief, he turned his phone on vibrate, but he unintentionally put it on silence. The mayor was noticeably upset, and he wasn't really paying attention to what the chief was saying.

The chief asked him if he was all right and if there was something wrong. He said, "You're not acting normal."

The mayor said, "It's my son. We haven't been able to find him."

The chief asked, "Have you called the hospital?"

He said, "Yes, but they don't have anybody with his name."

The chief said, "I know that you don't want to hear this, but have you call the coroner? We arrested three young black men for the beating death of a man last weekend."

The mayor broke down and sobbed with the thought of his son being dead. The mayor begin to call on the Lord to have mercy. "Oh! God, please don't let my son be dead. Oh! No!"

The chief said, "I can take you over there to identify the body."

The mayor was a Christian man, and he had compassion for the men that were locked up in jail on misdemeanor charges. But this was about his son, and he was in no mood to show any compassion

FORGIVENESS IS NOT AS HARD AS YOU MAKE IT

to the men who killed his son. He said, "Before we go, I want to see the young men that were arrested for this hideous crime."

They went to the jail, and when the mayor saw the three men, he just stood there not saying a word. They were in a group praying. After about two or three minutes, the mayor turned and walked away.

Before the mayor saw the young men, he was very angry, but after he saw them, he was perplexed by what he saw. In the mayor's heart, he felt that they were not men who would take another's man life. But he kept his thoughts to himself.

The chief of police was shocked that the mayor did not display any anger toward those young men.

The mayor said, "Let us go see who it is that they have in the morgue."

As they were leaving, the chief asked him if he was okay. The mayor replied, "Yes, let us just go and get this over with."

As they were driving to the morgue, the chief didn't know what to say because he couldn't tell if the mayor was angry or not.

The mayor told the chief, 'There is too much crime going in this city. And we need to put a stop to it. I need you and your staff to put a plan together and come to my office by next week. My Staff and I will come up with a plan as well."

Chapter 12

In the meantime, the mayor's secretary had been calling him for the last two hours, and he had not answered his phone. She called the chief's phone as well, and he had not answered his phone. The mayor and the chief forgot that they had put their phones on silence when they were in their meeting.

They arrived at the coroner's building, and as they entered, they were greeted by the receptionist. "Hi, Mr. Mayor, and Chief, how are you sir? What brings you out this way?"

"We're fine. We would like to speak to Frank." Frank Canova was the coroner for the county.

"Okay sir, if you would wait right here, I will get him for you." So the receptionist paged Dr. Frank Canova over the intercom to extension 2178.

Dr. Canova called back, "Hello!"

"Doctor, the mayor and the chief of police are here, and they are wanting to speak to you."

"Okay, tell them to have a seat, and that I will be on my way there."

Dr. Canova arrived. "Hi, mayor. Hello, chief. What brings you on this side of town?"

The mayor said, "I hear that you have a John Doe that came in this week, and I would like to see him."

Dr. Canova said, "I'm sorry, mayor, we did have a John Doe, but he was identified by family members. We researched his dental records to find his next of kin, and they took the body with them to be buried yesterday."

"Well, that's a relief. What was the cause of death?" The mayor asked.

"He was in a motor vehicle accident, and he had a lot of internal injuries," Dr. Canova replied. Dr. Canova asked the mayor what did he mean when he said, "That's a relief."

The mayor said, "My son is missing. So I came here to identify the body to see if he was my son. The whole time on my way here, I was praying that he was not my son. I'm sorry for his family's lost, but I am relieved that he is not my son. Okay, chief, let's head back across town."

When the chief and the mayor got back into the car, the mayor said to the chief, "When we get back to the jail, I guess you will have to release those young men and drop the charges."

"Mayor, we haven't found your son. I would hate to let them go, and they may be responsible for your son's disappearing—we don't know."

The mayor told the chief that that was wrong. He should let them go. "I don't believe that they had anything to do with my son's disappearing. I have that gut feeling." The chief and the mayor were going back and forth trying to justify their reasons. The mayor said, "At this point, you have no reason to hold them."

So the chief said to the mayor, "I will release them tomorrow afternoon. I just want to make sure that we are doing the right thing."

The mayor noticed that he had not received any phone call in the last four hours. That was very unusual. He was usually receiving calls every five to ten minutes. So he took out his cellphone and realized that his phone was on silent.

He forgot to turn it back on after his and the chief's meeting was over. He also noticed that he had missed fifteen calls and had only 5 percent battery charged. When he tried to use his phone, it turned off because the battery was so low.

The chief checked his phone, and he had 8 percent battery life on his phone. The chief got a call over the radio from the dispatcher. "Chief, we have been calling you for over an hour. Is the mayor with you?"

"Yes, he is."

"Let the mayor know that the hospital is trying to get in touch with him. They won't tell us why. When he gets back to the office, he needs to call the hospital administrator."

"Okay, we are on our way. By the way, our cellphone batteries are low, and they are charging."

The mayor commented to the chief, "I wonder what this is all about. The administrator might want me to be a part of some fundraiser event. Too bad my phone is not working. I would call him instead of going over there." The mayor asked the chief to take him to his car so that he could go to the office to catch up on all his missed calls. He didn't seem to be in a big hurry. All he had on his mind was where his son could be. *He may have called the office. Maybe he is lying in a ditch somewhere and nobody can find him. I don't know what to think.*

Chapter 13

Meanwhile, Kelvin was sitting on side of his bed in jail with his head down in his hands, crying. He was seriously thinking about the conversation that he and Kenneth had. Kenneth noticed him, but he didn't say anything to him because he thought that he might need some alone time. Kelvin knew that he had been doing things against God's will. He had been trying to run from God for a long time. No matter where he turned, he was convicted by God. Now that he was locked up, he had nowhere to run.

Kelvin came from a well-respected family who loved him. He had two younger siblings. As Kelvin was sitting on the side of his bed, he started think about when his life started to change.

He grew up going to church, and he enjoyed going when he was growing up. When he got older, he started hanging out with a few young men who were always getting into trouble with the law. They were guys he knew in high school. He started hanging out one or two times a week with them. They started flashing money in his face and telling him that he could make the same money if he would hang out with them more often and on the weekend.

The money looked good to him, so he tried it. What he had to do to make money didn't feel right to him. But the more he did it, the less it bothered him. Then they convinced him to use. He was reluctant to do so because it wasn't how he was raised. He knew what he was doing was wrong, but he did it anyway. His friends introduced him to marijuana. When he tried it, he didn't feel any affect from it, so he figured he would not get hooked on it. His friends kept pushing it on him, and he kept using it. Before he knew it, he was craving it more and more.

Kelvin knew that he loved the Lord, but the lure of the fast life pulled him farther and farther away from God. He didn't realize that the farther he thought he was away from God, God never left him.

Kelvin went deeper and deeper into the streets and deeper into sin. He started indulging in alcohol, drugs, and women. He rebelled against his family. He started lying and stealing. His parents tried to talk with him to turn him around. But he wouldn't listen to them. He had gotten to a point where all he wanted to do was to get high. He said some things to his parent that were so hurtful and disrespectful, it brought his mom to tears, and her heart was truly broken. He knew that she loved him so much. He knew that she was shocked by what he said to her. She always thought that out of all her children, she and Kelvin had a close relationship, and nothing could come between them.

As Kelvin sat on the side of that bed, the tears began to pour. His heart was heavy. The more he thought about how he broke his mother's heart and the things he said to her, the more he sobbed, tears flowing from his eyes like a river overflowing its banks. He could not stop crying. As Kelvin was crying and sobbing, he was also praying and repenting. He was asking God to forgive him for his sins. He asked God to save him.

"God, help me to overcome my addiction. God, help me to get back into my mother's grace." He didn't care who was looking at him. All he could think about was the pain he caused his family. This was the first time in three years that he had given this any serious thought. Kelvin knew from this point on that he had to make a change. He said to himself, *When I get out this time, I will reach out to my family and ask for forgiveness, especially to my mom.*

Kenneth gave Kelvin a few minutes to compose himself before he said anything else to him. Kenneth asked Kelvin, "Hey, man, are you okay?"

He replied, "I will be, and thanks for asking."

Kelvin had a lot on his heart. Kenneth told him to look him up when he got out. Kenneth told him the name of his church and that he could find him there and if he needed to talk, the pastor was a great listener.

Kelvin said, "Man, it's going to be a minute before I get out of here, and I don't want to make you any promises right now." Kelvin sighed. "Oh, God." He rubbed his head with both hands to compose himself.

Kelvin was unaware that God was already moving in his favor. He didn't know that his mom prayed for him night and day. His mom would say a prayer every morning and every night.

In the morning, she would say, "Lord, protect my son, keep him safe, keep your loving arms around him, let him know that he is loved." At night, she would say, "Lord, thank you for protecting my son. Lord, I haven't received any bad news about my son. I know that he is all right." Kelvin's mother never stopped loving her son. But he didn't know that.

A bailer came into the jail and called out Kelvin's name. Kelvin replied, "Yes sir."

The bailer said, "Let's go, your bail has been posted."

Kelvin looked shocked and totally surprised, and he was. Kelvin asked, "Who posted my bail?" The bailer said he didn't know.

As the bailer walked by Jackie's cell, Jackie asked him if anybody came by to post their bail. He said no.

Jackie, Sam, and Kenneth were getting a little discouraged, but they had to keep their spirits up.

As Kelvin was walking out, the bailer said to him, "Young man, this is not a place for you. God has His hands on you, and you keep pushing Him away. You have another chance to get it right. I saw you in that jail, pouring your heart out to God, and I believe He heard your cry. It is now time for you to make a change so that you can do what God wants you to do. You can be a big help to others. You need to stop thinking about yourself."

Kelvin heard what the jailer was saying. He said, "Yes sir." But he was trying to figure out who posted his bail.

When he reached the outside of the jail, there was a taxi waiting on him to take him wherever he wanted to go. The taxi driver drove him to a city park. He got out of the car, went and sat on a bench.

There he stayed for the rest of the day, thinking about all that he had been through. He knew that if he wanted to make a change in his life, he would have to stop hanging with his old friends and start doing the right thing. He had to get his life back on the right track so that he could prove to his mother that he has changed. He couldn't prove it to her until he proved it to himself.

So he set out looking for a good job. While he was looking for a job, he was in the neighborhood where his mother lived. He decided to go tell his mother that he has changed and that he was off drugs. He was getting his life together.

He got to the front door and rang the doorbell. His mother came to the door and asked, "Who is it?"

Kelvin says, "Mom, it's me."

She opened the door part way and looked at him. She says, "Boy, what do you want? What are you doing here? We don't have any money for you, and you can't come in. Go on back out there with your friends. Why did you come back here?"

He says, "But ma—"

She didn't give him a chance to say a word. She was angry but more hurt. She closed the door in his face. He turned and walked away with his head down and crying.

She was on the other side of the door, crying her heart out. When she saw him, she wanted to put her arms around him and love him like she did when he was a little baby. But she felt like she had to be tough with him no matter how hard it was on her.

Kelvin kept on walking, and he kept saying, "I am not going to give up on my mom like she has given up on me."

Chapter 14

Now when the chief returned to his office, he called the DA's office to talk about dropping the charges on Sam, Kenneth, and Jackie. When he called, the DA was out of town and the deputy DA was in court all day. He left a message with the deputy assistant for the deputy DA to give him a call. The assistant told him that it would be late in the day before he would be able to return his call.

The chief said, "Fine." The chief, seated behind his desk, proceeded to fill out the paper work to release the young men. The chief called the mayor to tell him that he has started the process to release the young men as he requested.

As the mayor and the chief was talking, the mayor's secretary chimed in on him and said to the mayor, "The hospital administrator is on the line."

The mayor said to her, "Tell him that I will return his call in a few minutes."

She said, "Sir, he has been calling you all day, and he sounds like it's urgent that he speak with you. I think that you should take the call now."

The mayor told her to put him on hold, and he will pick up. The mayor told the chief that he had to take this call.

The chief said, "Okay, and I will put a look out for your son and try to keep it out of the media."

The mayor hung up with the chief and pushed the wrong button on the phone to answer the call from the administrator and cut him off. "Oh my God, I just hung up on him," said the Mayor.

"Margret, I just hung up on Don Shaffer, the hospital administrator. Can you get him back on the line please?"

"Yes, sir. Oh, by the way, your wife called. She said she has been calling your son Conner for two days, and she is getting worried about him. She wanted to know if you had heard from him. It is not like him to not return her calls."

"Okay, I will call her a little later." The mayor sat at his desk with his head down in both hands, dreading that call. He had been keeping this quiet because he didn't want it to get out into the media, and he didn't want his wife to find out on the television.

His wife had a nervous condition. She worried all the time, she was battling depression, and she was taking antianxiety medication. The last thing that he wanted to do is upset her. He had been holding out from telling her that he couldn't find him either, but if he could hold out a little longer from telling her, maybe something will change, and he would be able to give her some good news. The mayor had his hands full. He was worried about the crime in the city, his wife and her condition, and he couldn't find his son.

He looked up toward the heavens and said, "Lord, why am I going through so much?"

His secretary told him that she called Mr. Shaffer, but he was not in the office. "Sir, the chief is on the other line."

"Okay, I'll get it. Hello chief, what's going on?"

"Mayor, we have a crisis on our hands. There was a bank robbery downtown, and one person has been shot."

"What bank is it?" the mayor asked.

"First National Bank on the corner of 57th and Main Street."

"Okay, I'll meet you down there." The mayor said to Margret that he had to go downtown. There had been a bank robbery.

As the mayor walked out of his office into that reception area, the hospital administrator walked in. He and the mayor looked at each other. Before Mr. Shaffer could say anything, the mayor spoke up, "Don, I know you called earlier, and I apologize for cutting you off. It was an accident, and Margret tried to call you back. I would love to talk to you about the fundraiser, but right now, I have a city crisis on my hand. There was a bank robbery and a person is injured and I need to go downtown to get a handle on things before they get out of hand."

"But mayor—" Don said.

The mayor cut him off. "Don, as soon as this is over, I will call you and come by your office, and we can discuss it then. Right now, I have to go."

Don said, "Mayor, just give me two minutes of your time. Just two minutes."

The mayor said, "Okay, two minutes."

"Sir, this is not about some fundraiser that is obvious you don't want to do. I have been calling you concerning your son."

"*My son?* What do you mean? Why are you calling me about my son?"

Don asked him, "Has your son been missing?"

"Ah yes," the mayor replied with a surprise look on his face, "but no one knows that. And why do you ask? I have been keeping it private because I didn't want it out in the media. What do you know about my son? Do you know where he is?"

Don replied, "We have your son in the hospital under the name of John Doe 459. We have been trying to identify him since he came into the hospital. One of the employees identified him and said that he is your son."

"But I called the hospital and I was told you didn't have him there," the mayor says.

"You may have, but he wasn't listed under his name. Therefore, we had no way of knowing that he is your son."

"How is he? What's wrong with him?" the mayor asked.

"He is in serious condition, and he is on a vent."

"What happened to him?"

"We don't really know, but he had a lot of trauma to his chest. We think that he will make it. We are doing all that we can for him."

"There are so many questions, and I can't believe that this is happening," the mayor said. "I—I—I got to go see him! I—I got to be with him."

Don said, "Let's go. I'll drive you and I can take you anywhere else you want to go. I don't think that you should drive in your state of mind."

Margret said, "I'll call your wife and let her know."

"No, no, don't do that just yet. She doesn't know that he was missing. Let me see him first, and I'll call you to send a car to pick her up. She will have a nervous breakdown if you call her." The mayor's eyes were red as he was fighting to hold back the tears.

As the mayor was leaving, in his mind, he was thanking God that his son was still alive. On the way out, the mayor called the chief of police to let him know about his son and ask him to handle the situation.

Chapter 15

At this time, the assistant DA returned to his office early. He was given the paperwork the chief had sent over to release Jackie, Sam, and Kenneth for lack of evidence and for new evidence that they were not the cause of a man's death.

The chief stated that they were not involved in the death of anyone and they should be released. He explained that he spoke to the coroner and found that the man that died was involved in an automobile accident and he wasn't beaten. So the DA looked over all the paperwork and the evidence that was before him and agreed that they should let them go.

As he was about to call the jailer to have them released, the pastor stepped into the DA's office requesting to post their bail. Before the DA could speak, the pastor started to talk about what good young men they are and how they had turned their life around. "There is no way that those young men could have done such a thing that they are being charged for. I am here to post their bail and take them home."

The DA said, "Hold on, pastor. There is no need for bail. I was just about to call the jailer to release them, and since you are here, you can take them home."

While all of that was going on, Kenneth said to Jackie, "Man, I'm ready to get out here."

Jackie, not knowing what was about to happen, said, "Hold on and be patient. God has not forgotten us. He will come through for us."

A few minutes later, the jailer called their names. To their surprise, he told them that it was time to go. "Your ride is here to pick you up."

They stood there and looked at each other. The jailer came as soon as Jackie got the words out of his mouth. Kenneth wanted to know what was going on and who it was that was there to pick them up.

Sam said, "I don't care who it is. I have had enough of this place. Let's go."

When they had gathered all of their things, they went to the front and there they met their pastor. Kenneth told him, "Pastor, I am glad to see you. Thank you so much for bailing us out."

The pastor grabbed them and hugged tightly. He said, "I didn't bail you out."

"What do you mean, pastor? How did we get out?" Sam said.

The pastor said, "I came here to post bail for you, and when I talked with the assistant DA, he told me that the charges were dropped for lack of evidence. So my timing was good, but God's plan was great."

Kenneth shouted, "*Thank you, Jesus!* Now let's go and get out of here. I want to take a good long bath and see my baby."

When they were on their way home, they called their jobs and explained what had happened. Their supervisors told them that they still had a job. They were so relieved. They really believed that God was looking out for them.

On the way home, the pastor was explaining to them what the DA had told him. The person that died was not the man that they helped, and they were still looking for him.

Jackie said, 'We took him to the hospital, so what happened to him from there?"

"I believe he is still there."

He asked the pastor, "How can we find out his name? I would like to go see him."

The pastor said, "I have a connection at the hospital, and I will see what I can find out. I should have an answer by tomorrow."

Chapter 16

As the mayor was on his way to the hospital, his mind was running away. He was wondering what his son was doing to get himself in this condition. *Who did this to him? Whoever did this is going to pay dearly.*

Don was explaining his son's condition, and he was doing well in spite of how he may look. "He is in serious condition."

"Do you think that he is going to die?" the mayor asked.

"Mayor, let's not think on that right now."

The mayor sat quietly looking out the window of the car with tears streaming down his face. He couldn't say another word.

Don called out, "Mayor, are you okay?" But he didn't reply.

They arrived at the hospital. The mayor just sat there in the car, not moving. He was preparing himself for what his son may look like. Don took him into a private entrance to keep people from seeing him.

As they made it to ICU to Conner's room, the mayor stopped at the door, staring at his son with tubes in and out of his body. He had never seen so many IV tubes and wires in a person. As he walked closer to his son, he couldn't hold the tears back any longer. He reached out and grabbed his hand. He couldn't say a word, he just stood there with tears flowing down his cheeks, like water flowing down the side of a mountain.

He bent over and kissed his son on his forehead. He whispered to him, "I love you son."

As he sobbed and wept, the staff were in the background, crying along with him. He was looking around at the tubes and listening to the sound of the monitor—*beep! beep! beep! beep! beep!*

The tears would not stop flowing. He tried to pull himself together as he said a little prayer under his voice, "God, oh my God, please hear my prayer. I come to you, oh mighty God, not just on my behalf but my son as well. I know that I haven't done anything so great to deserve your goodness. But I do know that you are a God of mercy, a God of forgiveness, a God of compassion, and I am asking you to have mercy and compassion on my son. He is my only son, and I love him so much. Please don't take him away. Heal him, Lord, and make him well. I believe in you and I know that you can and you are able."

He still could not stop sobbing. A nurse came over with tears in her eyes, and she put her hand on his shoulder. When she did that, he turned and laid his head in the laps of her shoulder and sobbed even more. She was surprised that he did that because he was the mayor of the city. Then she thought, *He is human too. He is a person who need a shoulder to cry on and someone to care.*

As they stood there, other nurses showed compassion and hugged him as well. They walked the mayor to a chair to sit him down. The patient's nurse took him by the hand and told him that his son is going be okay as she wiped the tears from her eyes. Another nurse brought tissue over and gave it to the nurse and the mayor.

"We have him sedated so that he can heal. We are doing every-thing to make him comfortable and to get him better. He is doing very well. He has come long way, and he is getting better."

After a few minutes, the mayor said, "Thank you for your kind-ness. I will be all right now. I'm sorry for carrying on like this. Seeing my son like this got the best of me." The mayor composed himself, got up, and went back to his son's bedside. At that time, the doctor came into the room.

"Hello, mayor, are you related to him?"

"Yes, this is my son."

The doctor was shocked to learn this. "I'm sorry about your son, but he is improving very well. I would like to start the process of getting him off this vent. So we will start reducing the sedation drip to wake him up and if he responds well, we will take him off the vent and hope to send him home soon."

The mayor said, "Who would do this to another human being? Whoever did this, I am going to see that they pay."

The doctor said to him, "Three young men brought him in the emergency room a few days ago. I don't know if they captured them or not. And I don't know if they had anything to do with his condition. But it is a good thing that they brought him in when they did or he would be dead. He is improving very well."

After the mayor heard all what the doctor had said, he was grateful. After being with his son and finding out that he was going to be all right, he thought about his wife and how she was going to handle it. He decided to leave his son to go tell his wife personally. It was hard for him to leave, but he knew that his son was getting the best of care.

Chapter 17

By now, all of Conner's friends had heard that he was in the hospital. They were relieved that he was not dead and happy that he was alive. So they all met up at the hospital—all but one: Tyler.

Tyler had heard that Conner was in the hospital because he received the same text that his friends had received, but he was too ashamed to go see Conner. He didn't know how serious Conner's condition was. He felt like Conner would hate him. He felt like what Conner was going through was his fault. His guilt was so strong, he knew that he could not be forgiven. He and Conner were very close, and he let his petty anger destroy their relationship. He would do anything to get that relationship back, but he felt like Conner would never forgive him.

Mark texted Tyler: *Hey man, we are at the hospital checking on Conner, where are you? You do know that he is here, right?*

Tyler saw the text but refused to respond.

Hey, man, call me. Why won't you reply?

To deal with his problem and to numb the pain, he went to the liquor store. He knew that this was not the right way to deal with problems, but he felt like he had nowhere to turn and no one to talk to. If he told his friends the truth, they would turn on him too.

He bought a fifth of vodka and headed to the city park. He hadn't opened the bottle, but it was in his back pocket. As he walked around in the park, he heard voices in his head and they were about to drive him crazy. He was dealing with fear and worrying about what his friends would do when they find out that Conner was sick because of him.

Will they reject me? I will be an outcast. How did I mess up so bad? Not just my life but Conner's as well. I must be the worst person ever. Tyler didn't realize that the devil was filling his head with confusion.

As he was walking, he felt that bottle in his back pocket. He pulled it out and looked at it. It was tempting, but he said, "Not now."

The devil kelp telling him to go ahead and take a sip. *It will make you feel better.*

But Tyler kept saying, "No, not now." He was thinking how alcohol did his father, and he did not want to end up like his father.

But the devil kept nudging him. *You won't end up like him, it's only one sip. Go ahead and it will make you forget what you did to your friend.*

The more Tyler thought, the more confused he got. He saw a bench in the park and no one was on it. He sat on the bench with his head down, eyes full of tears, runny nose, no friends, no family and no one to talk too. He felt so alone in this world. He didn't know what to do.

Chapter 18

Kelvin had been looking for a job since he got out of jail. He had been in jail long enough to get sober, clean, and made up his mind to stay sober and clean. He ran across a couple of old friends.

"Hey, Kelvin. You got something, man?"

"No, man. I stopped doing drugs. I can't do that no mo."

"Aw man, come on, we can get some dope."

Kelvin said, "No man, ya'll go on. I got things to do."

"What you got to do? You ain't got no job. Ain't nobody gone hire you."

Kelvin was frustrated because he couldn't find a good job. No factories would hire him because of his record. Kelvin said to himself, *I know I messed up. No one will give me a second chance.*

All he wanted to do was get a job so that he could get back into his mother's grace. He longed for his mother's love. He felt that he had to prove to her that he has changed for the better. As he was walking back into the city park, where he has been sleeping, he saw a man working on a lawn mower. Something had gotten stuck in the blades and it wouldn't start.

Kevin started walking toward him, and the man looked up and saw him coming his way.

The man said to himself, *Oh my God, here come this homeless man coming to ask me for some money. I ain't got no money to give them people to get drunk and high. He should find a job. I got my own family to feed.*

Kelvin approached the man. "Excuse me, sir…"

Before Kelvin could ask the man for what he wanted, the man cut him off. "I ain't got no money and I can't help you."

Kelvin's feelings were hurt, but he had to put his feelings to the side. He knew how people saw him as he looked on the outside. On the inside, he knew that he was better than what people thought of him. But he couldn't give up. He remembered the words of encouragement Kenneth gave to him in jail.

Kelvin said, "Sir, I'm not here to ask you for money. I come to ask you for a job. I want to work, I want to change my circumstance."

The man felt small and ashamed. He couldn't believe that Kelvin was looking for a job. The man told Kelvin no, he's not hiring.

Kelvin pleaded with the man. "I will do any job that you have." The man still said no.

Kelvin turned to walk away, and he said under his breath, "God, give me another chance. Open a door for me, give me a job no matter how big or small. I need your help."

The man got back onto his lawn mower, but it wouldn't start. Kelvin turn around and saw that the man was a bit frustrated. So Kelvin went back to the man and said, "Sir, can I take a look at it?"

The man said, "Do you know something about lawn mowers?"

Kelvin said, "A little." He looked at it and put a wire back on that had come off. He said, "See if it will start now." The lawn mower started up.

The man said, "Thank you. Now, how much are you going to charge me?"

Kelvin said, "Nothing, sir."

The man said, "Nothing. In this day and time nobody does something for nothing. So how much?"

Kelvin said, "Man, if we can't help each other without looking for something in return, what good are we?"

The man said, "You seem like a good fellow. I'll tell you what, can you be here tomorrow at 6:30 a.m.? I may have some work for you to do. It don't pay much. But if you are one minute late, don't bother about showing up."

Kelvin said, "Really! Thank you, sir. I will be here." Kelvin walked away with joy and hope in his heart and said, "Thank you, God, for answering my prayer." He was feeling like things were about to turn around for him.

Chapter 19

Kelvin headed back to the park bench that he was on the night before. When he got there, he saw a man sitting there with his head down. He thought that if he went and sat by this man, he would get up and leave. *No one wants to sit by a homeless, smelly man. And when he gets up, I can have the bench to myself.*

Kelvin sat on the other end of the bench, but the man paid him no attention. The man was sitting there, talking to himself and crying. Kelvin didn't know what to do. So he said to the man, "Excuse me, sir, I don't mean to pry, but are you alright?"

The man said, "No, I'm not. I feel like just ending it all."

Kelvin says, "Man, I don't know what you are going through, but whatever it is, it can't be that bad. Why would you want a permanent solution to a temporary problem?"

He said, "You just don't know."

Kelvin said, "No, I don't know, but what I do know is where God has brought me from. And I have been in some low places. I know that I am a homeless guy, but if you want someone to listen to you, I'm all ears because right now, you need a friend."

The man introduced himself. "My name is Tyler."

"My name is Kelvin. Nice to meet you."

Tyler asked him, "How can you talk about a God like you do and you're homeless? Why did your God put you in this condition?"

"He didn't," Kelvin said. "I used to be in the church, but I allowed people to push me out. Then I turned my back on God. But I realized He never turned his back on me. So let me ask you a question Mr. Tyler: why are you sitting on this bench with your head down and wanting to end your life? What are you running from?"

He said, "I turned my back on my best friend, and when I realized what I did, I couldn't find him. Now I hear that he is in the hospital and it's my fault. When he needed me, I wasn't there for him."

Tyler proceeded to tell him what happened. When he was done, he told Kelvin that he didn't think that his friend would ever forgive him.

Kelvin said, "That's what you think. You don't know what he is going to do. When you are thinking about what you believe he is going to do, it is what you would do if the shoe was on the other foot. What I'm saying is, if he would have done you wrong, you would not forgive him. So since you did your friend wrong, you think that he won't forgive you? Until you go see him and ask him for his forgiveness, you won't know what he will do. Don't beat yourself up. Put your fears to the side and go and apologize to him.

"Can I tell you something? I hurt my mom real bad. I broke her heart. She put me out and I've been on the streets since then. I felt so bad. I started hanging with the wrong kind of guys, using drugs, and getting high every day, drinking, and using bad language to hide from the pain. I did her wrong, and I beat myself up about it. I want my mother's love back. God knows that I do. God kept me when I wanted to give up. So I stopped trying to die and I stopped beating myself up. I started to want to live. I stopped feeling sorry for myself. I went to my mom's house, and she didn't give me a chance to tell her that I was sorry. She closed the door in my face. She saw the clothes that I have on, but she couldn't see my heart. I'm not bitter at her. But I still have hope that she will forgive me one day.

"You know, if I would have killed myself, then I would never know if she forgave me and I would not know that she loves me. I believe in my heart that she still loves me. I didn't do this on my own. I was in jail, and a stranger talked to me and he prayed for me and with me. He lit my torch that went out a long time ago. Now that it is burning, I must stay prayed up to keep the fire burning. I had to ask God to forgive me and then I had to forgive myself and now I am working to get my mother to forgive me.

"You see, not only you have a story to tell, I bet you that everybody in this park has a story to tell. You can't just give up because of how you think that someone feels about you. You have to show love to them no matter what."

Tyler said to him, "Man, you are a very smart man. What are you doing out here? I would have never thought that of you if I would have walked past you."

Kelvin said, "Man, people think that all homeless people are people that don't have a soul and a heart. There are a lot of them who care about other people. They are people who fell on hard times. Some of it was their own fault and some of it wasn't their fault. A lot of these people are smart people who are just down on their luck. Granted, there are a lot of them out here who are on drugs and alcohol. I was one of them, but my God has delivered me from that. He has given me another chance."

Tyler said, "Talking to you has made me feel better. I'm not happy about what I did. You keep talking about this God of yours. I don't understand. I believe that there is a higher power. I have never been to a church, and I never had anyone talk to me about this God you are talking about."

Kelvin said, "Mr. Tyler, I can't make you believe. I can tell you this: I wouldn't want to die and never know God as my personal Savior. If you want to know him, it is not too late. If you want to know Him, you should surround yourself with people who know Him, so that they can teach you the love of Jesus Christ. You have to believe for yourself. If you believe in God, you should form a personal relationship with Him. I must tell you this: just because you believe and trust in him, that doesn't mean that you will not have trouble in your life. But once you do believe and trust in Him, you will be better able to deal with it.

"I believe that our paths crossed because it was God's plan for us to meet. Here we are as strangers—I'm homeless and you are not. I'm black and you're white, and yet we are having a conversation with mutual respect. If God did not plan this, we would not have met. You should have a talk with God and get to know Him and ask Him to forgive you of your sins. Then you will need to forgive yourself. Then you should go to your friend and ask him to forgive you. Maybe your friend will forgive you, I don't know. Don't do this because I said so, search your heart and let God lead you to do the right thing. I see that you have that bottle in your hand."

Tyler said, "Yes, I was planning on drinking it. I want to stop the pain."

"If you are planning to drink that to ease your pain or to make you forget your troubles, I must tell you that it won't work. Look at me and the shape that I'm in. I did what you are about to do and look where it got me. Man, that bottle is not the answer. The answer is to repent of your sins and believe in your heart that God is there to help you get through your pain and through your troubles."

Even though Kelvin had stopped drinking, when he saw that bottle, the taste had come back to his mouth. In his mind, he said to himself, *I refuse to give up now. I have to regain my mother's trust and love. I can't do it if I'm drunk.*

Tyler said to him, "You know, Mr. Kelvin, I really want to thank you for helping me. You saved my life and I am grateful to you. I've got to go, and I hope to see again."

Kelvin said, "Man, don't thank me. God gets the glory, for it was He who put this meeting together. I'm just thankful that He is using me. One day we will meet again."

When Tyler left, Kelvin sat on that bench and dwelled on the conversation that he just had with Tyler. He began to meditate on God's word and what the jailer told him as he was leaving. *Let God use you and stop running away from him.*

As he sat there, he felt like God was going to turn things around in his favor. He felt like he did what God wanted him to do, and he knew that he had more work to do. He hadn't talked about God like this in a long time and it made him feel good on the inside. As it began to get dark, he said a prayer for Tyler and for himself. He didn't know if he was going to see Tyler any more, but he hoped that he would give his life to God.

Kelvin laid down on that bench for the night, knowing that he had to get up early for his new job. He was excited. He didn't want to be late. He didn't realize that he had sown a seed.

Chapter 20

The pastor had called Jackie to tell him that he found out about the young man that they took to the hospital and his name was Conner. "He is the mayor's son." He said, "Call Kenneth and Sam, and I will meet you all at the hospital."

They arrived at the hospital within a few minutes of each other and gathered in the hospital front lobby. Sam asked the pastor, "What if we can't see him? Then what?"

The pastor said that he had privileges and he was allowed to visit patients and he could bring support with him.

They went up to Conner's room, and when they saw him, they couldn't believe that he was the same guy that they brought to the emergency room. There were so many IVs, tubes going everywhere, and monitors with different sounds going off. They stood by his bedside, looking and staring. There was so much to take in.

Jackie whispered to Kenneth, "I didn't know that he was in this bad of a condition."

"Me neither," he replied.

After visiting for a few minutes, the pastor called them together to pray. They hovered around Conner's bed and joined hands, and Kenneth said to the pastor, "I will pray."

When they were done praying, a nurse walked into the room and asked if they knew him.

Sam said, "Not really, we are the ones that brought him to the emergency room, and we are here to see how he is doing."

She said, "It is a good thing that you brought him in when you did. If not, he would have died. He is doing well in spite of the way he looks."

They felt better in knowing that he will be alright, but they could not comprehend how he got in this condition and what caused this.

They began to leave Conner's room, and on the way out, the mayor was coming in. The mayor noticed the four men coming out of his son's room. He knew the pastor, and he knew that he knew the three young men from somewhere, but he couldn't place them.

The pastor greeted the mayor and shook hands. The pastor said to the mayor, "We just came out of your son's room, and we had prayer for him. By the way, these young men who are with me are from the church."

The mayor shook their hands. As he shook their hands, he stared at them as if he knew them. The mayor asked Jackie, "Have we met before?"

And Jackie said, "No sir, I don't believe so." Jackie, Kenneth, and Sam did not see the mayor when he saw them in the jail.

The mayor asked them, "Are you friends with my son Conner?"

Jackie said, "No sir, not really."

"What do you mean 'not really'?"

Kenneth stepped in and said, "Sir, we are the ones who brought him to the emergency room. We didn't know what happened to him. We were stopped in traffic, and he asked us to take him to the hospital."

"Were you the guys that were in jail?"

"Yes sir," Jackie said.

"I knew that I have seen you before." the mayor said.

Jackie told the mayor, "We were falsely accused of beating someone to death. We were assumed guilty without any evidence and locked up, not because of who we are today but because of who we were. I am not complaining, because we know that God is for us, no matter who is against us."

The mayor says, "I was told that you were the ones that were responsible for my son's death, and I went to jail with anger and hatred in my heart. I wanted to confront you and punish you for what I was told and believed you did. But when I saw you in jail praying over a young man, God put in my heart that you all were not the ones responsible for my son."

Sam said, "Mayor, we did not harm your son. All we tried to do was to do the right thing—help a brother in need regardless of his race. If we are to be disciples for Jesus, we can't allow race or our differences stop us from helping one another.

"Even though we were locked up for something that we didn't do, it wasn't a lost cause. In that jail, six people gave their life to Christ, and we are happy to be a part of that. We didn't want to be there, but it wasn't in our control."

"The doctor told me that if you had not brought him to the hospital, he would have died, and for that I am grateful," said the mayor. "If there is anything that you need, please give me a call. Here is my personal cellphone number." The mayor gave each of them a business card with his cellphone number on the back of it. "Please call me day or night."

"Yes, sir, Mr. Mayor," said Jackie.

Chapter 21

Tyler was home sitting on the couch, feeling depressed, angry, guilty, and sad. The apartment was totally quiet. He kept thinking about the things the homeless man told him. He forgot his name, but he remembered him talking about God. The silence in the apartment was making matters worse for him. His mind was getting the best of him. A whole lot of "what ifs." So much confusion going on in his head. He just wanted to end it all.

To get rid of the silence, he turned on the TV just to have some noise in the apartment. As he set there, he flipped through the channels, and he couldn't find anything interesting to look at. As much as he loved sports, he didn't want to watch them. He flipped through the channels very fast until he ended up back at the beginning. He got up and went to the kitchen, not realizing that he left the channel on a Christian network.

He was getting a beer out of the refrigerator when he heard a man's voice on the TV say, "No matter what you are going through, God loves you and He will help you get through your storm."

That got his attention. He walked back into the room where the TV was and sat down on the couch with the beer in his hand, unopen. He sat there, focused on every word that the man was speaking.

The man said, "When you think that you are all alone, you're not. Jesus is with you. Call on His name and you will receive His comfort. When you think that no one cares or love you, Jesus cares, and He loves you. He is there with open arms waiting to receive you. All you have to do is let Him into your heart."

The man started reading scriptures from Isaiah 43 (NIV):

> But now, this is what the Lord says—he who cre-
> ated you, Jacob, he who formed you, Israel:
> "Do not fear, for I have redeemed you; I
> have summoned you by name; you are mine.
> When you pass through the waters, I will
> be with you;
> and when you pass through the rivers, they
> will not sweep over you.
> When you walk through the fire, you will
> not be burned; the flames will not set you ablaze.
> For I am the Lord your God, the Holy One
> of Israel, your Savior;
> I give Egypt for your ransom, Cush[a] and
> Seba in your stead.
> Since you are precious and honored in my
> sight, and because I love you,
> I will give people in exchange for you,
> Nations in exchange for your life.
> Do not be afraid, for I am with you; I will
> bring your children from the east and gather you
> from the west.
> I will say to the north, 'Give them up!' and
> to the south, 'Do not hold them back.'
> Bring my sons from afar and my daughters
> from the ends of the earth—
> everyone who is called by my name, whom I
> created for my glory, whom I formed and made."
> Lead out those who have eyes but are blind,
> who have ears but are deaf.

"God is telling you that He created you and you belong to him. No matter what you are going through—what rivers you have to cross, what fire you have to go through, what mountain you have to climb, what storm may come your way—if you just stay in the boat,

63

stay on course, don't give up, believe in Him, and trust Him, He will comfort you and He will protect you. He's got your back. Don't worry about the things that you did wrong. God will forgive you. Think about the good that you can do for others right now. It's up to you. Are you going to trust God and let Him help you in what you are going through?"

Tyler started to feel strange, as if this man was talking directly to him. Tyler had gotten up and walked back into the kitchen, opened the refrigerator and replaced that beer in his hand. He never did open it. Then he went back into the TV room and sat back down on the couch.

He was wondering what just happened. He took his phone out and looked up that scripture Isaiah 43 and read it over and over. After reading it the third time, he began to understand it a little better.

He sat there in silence for a few minutes, and then he said in a low voice, "God." It sounded strange to him because he never spoke to God before. He said, "God" again but a little louder. "God, I don't know you, but I want to get to know you. God, I don't know how to pray so I ask you to teach me how to pray. I am a sinner, and I ask you to save me from my sinful ways. I am a lost sheep who is without a shepherd. I want to give my life to you right now. I'm asking you to come into my life and redeem me. Forgive me, God, for all the wrong that I have done. Forgive me, God, for my selfish ways. Forgive me, God, for turning my back on my best friend when he needed me the most. Help me, oh God. My heart is heavy, God. Take the weight off my back, free me, oh God, from these shackles that bind me. Be my Lord and Savior, oh God, be my savior."

As Tyler prayed, the tears began to flow. He kept saying over and over, "Lord God, forgive me, forgive me, forgive me, Lord." As he kept repeating, he began to feel lighter. He was surprised to feel a change come over him so soon. Suddenly, he didn't feel so depressed. He began to have a little hope. He didn't know how to praise God for the change he was feeling. So he sat back on the couch and soaked it all in.

Tyler was talking to himself. He needed to build his nerves up to go see his friends, but he didn't want to go there when he had a lot of visitors. He figured he would go around the time visiting hours were over. Hopefully, his other friends will not be there, and he could have some alone time with Conner—plus he wouldn't have to explain why he didn't come around.

He didn't know Conner's condition, if he was able to talk or not. If Conner didn't want to forgive him for his mistake, then he would have to live with it. If Conner didn't, then he would work hard to make it up to him.

Tyler was going to go that night, but he got scared and changed his mind. His nerves got the best of him. He said, "I'll go tomorrow night."

The next day, Tyler was thinking about visiting Conner all day. His heart had been racing all day. The later it got in the evening, the more he began to sweat—his hands were sweaty as well.

Unbeknownst to Tyler, the doctor had taken Conner off the ventilator, but he was unable to speak. His family was there with him all day, but he was sleeping off and on. Conner had so many friends and family who loved him and supported him. The waiting room was full of his family and friends. The mayor was overwhelmed by the love and support for his son. All of Conner's best friends were there to support him except Tyler. They all noticed it. Tyrone said he tried to get in touch with Tyler, but he couldn't get an answer. The other fellows said that they had tried as well, and they didn't get an answer either.

It was getting late, and the mayor thanked everyone for coming out to support his son. He said, "My family and I are truly grateful for you to come out." He said, "It's getting late and we should go so that Conner can get some rest."

Fifteen minutes before visiting hours were over, everyone had left the hospital. Tyler walked into Conner's room after avoiding running into his friends. His heart was racing 110 beats per minute. He was perspiring profusely. Conner was laying there, asleep.

Tyler eased a chair next to his bed very quietly and sat in it, trying not to awake him. He was looking all around at the IV lines that were connected to Conner. He was very sad, his eyes were red, and the tears began to flow. He sat there with elbows resting on side of the bed, his hands clasped together as if he was praying.

He said to Conner in a low voice, "I'm very sorry for putting you through this. You are my best friend and I let you down." The tears were flowing heavy and uncontrollable. He could not stop crying. He was trying to be very quiet.

He said, "If I had listened to you and taken you to the hospital when you asked me to, you wouldn't be in this condition. This is my fault. It may be hard for you to forgive me, but I hope that you will find a way to forgive me. I love you, man, and I don't want to lose a friend. If you don't forgive me, I can truly understand why. I was selfish and angry for no reason. I don't know why I did what I did. We have been friends for a very long time. We have been in and out of trouble together, and we always stood by each other. I have always been there for you and you have done the same for me. I messed up. To see you like this, I know that it is my fault. This is my fault. This—is—my—fault."

He said this as he clutched his fist. "You are my brother and I don't want to lose that relationship that we have because of my stupid mistake. If you end up hating me, I will do whatever it takes to regain your trust. I love you, man, and I am hurt because of what I did to you."

Tyler put his head down with tears steadily dripping from his eyes. He said, "Please forgive me." He kept repeating, "Please forgive me. Forgive me."

About the fourth time he said that, Conner reached out and touched Tyler on his head as it was down on the bed. Tyler looked up at Conner as he tried to wipe away the tears from his face. He said, "Man, I'm so sorry."

Conner looked at him and gave him a thumbs-up as if to say it's okay. Tyler couldn't hold back the tears, he sobbed profusely and was relieved to know that he was forgiven. He started to explain his guilt, but Conner waved his hand as if to say, "No need to explain."

Conner patted Tyler on the hand as to say he was glad to see him. It was hard for Tyler to believe that Conner forgave him, but he thought about the conversation he had with the homeless guy. So he sat there with Conner until late into the night.

He said, "Thank you, God." He thought about what he just said. He realized at that point, he had changed. He never acknowledged God before. The change felt good. It was late in the night, so Tyler went home.

On the way home, he thought about the homeless man he talked with about God when he was at his lowest point. Tyler wanted to learn more about God. Since the homeless man knew so much about God and he was easy to talk to, Tyler felt the need to talk to him some more. The embarrassing part was he forgot his name, but he wasn't going to let that deter him. He just wanted to thank him for helping him when he was at his lowest point.

Each day that Tyler would go visit Conner in the hospital, after the visit, he would go to the park to see if he could find Kelvin. He didn't see him. He kept going back to that same bench in the park where they meet, but he still didn't see him. After a few days of not seeing Kelvin, Tyler began to wonder if something had happened to him.

Chapter 22

After a week had passed, Conner was doing a whole lot better. He was sitting up, eating and talking. The doctor was ready to release him. All his family and friends were there, including Tyler.

Tyrone asked Conner, "What happened to him?"

Tyler was getting very nervous. He was looking at Conner and Conner looked at him.

Conner said, "Do you remember the last game we played together?"

Tyrone said, "Yeah."

"Well, I thought that I may have pulled a muscle. When we got home, I took a shower, and when I was done, I told Tyler that I was going for a walk. When I left the apartment, the pain got worse. I thought that I was going to die. I remember asking some guys in a van that was stopped in traffic to take me to the hospital. After I got in the van, I don't remember anything else. I must have passed out."

Tyler was so relieved to hear what Conner had to say. He knew that Conner wasn't telling the whole story. He wasn't going to say anything about it. Conner avoided telling the whole truth because he didn't want his friends to hate Tyler and turn against him. At that point, Tyler realized what kind of true friend he really had.

Conner said to Tyler that he was going to stay with his parents until he is fully recovered. After a couple of months, he would come back to the apartment. He would still pay his part of the rent. Tyler nodded his head in agreement.

Every day when Tyler left the hospital after visiting Conner, he would go to the park to look for Kelvin. He couldn't find him. He kept going to the park day after day.

One day, he went to the park and sat on the beach where he met Kelvin. He sat there for almost two hours. A black man came and sat next to him. He was nicely dressed. Nothing fancy. His hair was freshly cut, and his beard was neatly trimmed. He was a very nice-looking man.

Tyler looked at the man and ask if he had seen a homeless man with long dreadlocks, a scraggly beard, and wearing loose-fitting clothes. He wore an old army hat. He said, "I'm looking for him because he saved my life, and I want to tell him how grateful I am."

The man said, "Are you Tyler?"

Tyler said, "Yes, I am. How do you know?"

The man said, "I'm Kelvin. I am the homeless guy you talked with. I am glad to see that you are doing better. Things must have worked out for you."

Tyler was totally surprised. He grabbed Kelvin and hugged him real tight and thanked him. He said, "Thank you, man, thank you so much." Tyler said, "What happened to you? You look so different."

Kelvin told him that the day that they had met, he was offered a job. He has been working since. Each time he got paid, he kept making improvements to do better. He said, "I'm still homeless, but I am saving to get me a place to stay. I work during the day and a few hours in the evening, I help out at the shelter. They let me stay in a small closet-like room in exchange for my help. I asked them if I could stay there just for a few of weeks until I get a place of my own. I mentor to the homeless there and give them hope in Jesus. God has been good to me and I must do His will."

Tyler said, "Man, I can't thank you enough. If you had not have taken the time to talk to me, I would have been dead. You saved my life. You talked to me about God and you opened my eyes. I have been looking for you every day. I want to learn more about God. I want to be a witness for him. I followed your advice about not to pre-judge what someone is going to say. I went to see my friend and I apologized to him, I asked for his forgiveness and he forgave me, and he didn't express any anger. I wasn't sure how he was going to react. I looked for you because I want to learn about the God that you talk about. I feel like I can learn a lot from you. I can talk to you and I like that."

Kelvin said, "That's fine with me. We can meet here once a week. Let's say Wednesday evening at 6 o'clock."

Tyler agreed.

"Maybe you can come with me to the shelter sometimes."

Tyler said, "Okay, I can do that."

After getting together for a couple of weeks, they had gotten to know each other very well, and they had started to trust each other. They were getting along like they had known each other for a very long time.

Tyler asked Kelvin how his apartment hunting was coming along. Kelvin said, "I'm saving some money to get one."

Tyler had an idea. Tyler said to Kelvin, "My roommate is staying with his parents for a little while, and his room is going to be vacant. I could talk to him to see if it would be all right if you could stay there, and maybe you can find an apartment before he is ready to return." Tyler had taken to Kelvin. He felt like their friendship had really grown, plus he felt compelled to help Kelvin in any way possible.

Kelvin says, "Man, I appreciate the offer, but I have to decline. Please don't take offense, I just like living alone."

Tyler said, "I just want to help you out." He says to Kelvin, "Man, before I met you, I was selfish and didn't care about anybody else's feelings—only mine. Then I found myself all alone, down and depressed. I was about to take my own life. You helped me see things in a different light. You taught me the word of God, so I just wanted to show you my appreciation."

Kelvin said, "Look, man, God allowed our paths to cross. You don't owe me. Someone helped me, so I helped you, and you will be a blessing to someone else. God wants us to come together and spread his word with love in our heart. Even though you're white and I'm black, I'm homeless and you're not, God wants us to reach out to each other, help one another, and most of all love one another."

Tyler said, "Then tell me how do we reach others? I want to do whatever I can."

Kelvin said, 'We build bridges and meet each other in the middle."

"Build bridges?" Tyler asked.

"Yes, we have to build a bridge over the things and people who are trying to hinder us from coming together and loving each other.

"Let me give you an example. Let's say that we are on the edge of a riverbank. There are black people who are believers of Jesus Christ, and there are white people on the other sides of the river who are believers of Christ. Both sides want to come together, but there is confusion and chaos between them. They are shouting at each other, and they can't hear what each side is saying because of the noise coming from the river. On one side of the river, they are saying, 'If only you could feel my pain.' But what they are hearing on the other side is, 'We are not the same.' What the other side is saying is, 'Reach out and grab my hand,' but what the other side is hearing, 'Why don't you go back to your homeland?'

"The river is flowing with hate, racism, envy, lies, and all the things that are against God's will. The river is growing at a fast rate and it is about to crest. The higher the river gets, the louder the noise gets. The people who are trying to make peace can't hear each other because of the noise coming from the river. Both sides of the river have family and friends in the river, and they don't want to anger them by not agreeing with them. The people on both sides of the river need to know that they as individuals have to give an account for their action to God. You shouldn't stand with someone when you know that they are wrong.

"When a bridge builder needs to build a bridge across a wide river, he starts on both sides of the river and meets in the middle. As we build this bridge, we must throw a lifeline to those who are in the river. Someone may want to get out of the river, but they don't have a lifeline to get out. As we build this bridge, we have to give others a chance to join in. However, before we can build a bridge, we have to find a way to talk to each other and know that we are not going to agree on everything."

Tyler said, "Man, how do you come up with this kind of thinking?"

"When you are homeless, you have a lot of time to think about things," Kelvin says. "When you're homeless, people look at you as if you are a piece of trash. You have no value. But they say that they love Jesus, and yet they don't realize that He was homeless too. Jesus is wanting to make a home in your heart, but how can He when you don't have any compassion for others?"

Tyler said to Kelvin, "Man, you are deep, and I have never had this kind of conversation with anyone before. I really like it. I am going to have to go now so that I can stop by Conner's before it gets too late. You have given me so much to think about."

"Okay, man, we'll talk later," Kelvin said.

Chapter 23

As Tyler approached Conner's parents' home, he noticed that there were a couple of cars parked in the front yard that didn't belonged to the mayor. He started to get anxious and nervous.

Is there something wrong with Conner? Did he have a relapse? His head started spinning with negative thoughts. As he approached the steps to the front porch, his nerves were getting the best of him. As he stepped on to the porch and he reached the front door, before he could knock, he heard them talking, but he couldn't make out what they were saying.

All of a sudden, he heard someone laugh out loud. He felt somewhat relieved but not completely. Now he was wondering what could be so funny.

He knocked on the door and Conner's father opened the door. He said, "Hi, Mr. Edenfield, how are you? Is Conner in?"

He said to Tyler, "Yes, he is and how are you? I'm good. I'm a little tried, but I'm okay. Come on in, I'm glad that you could join us."

When Tyler walked in, he saw Tyron and Danny sitting on a sofa, and there were three other men there that he didn't know. He reached out to Tyron and give him a handshake and a shoulder hug, and he did the same with Danny. "What's up fellows?"

Danny said, "Man, where have you been? You don't come around like you used too. You don't call. Are you alright?"

Tyler said, "Man, I have been going through some stuff and I had to get some things done. But I'm straight. I'm back." Tyler knew he was lying because he was still struggling with the fact that he let his best friend down, and he knew that one day they would know the truth why Conner was in the condition that he's in.

The mayor turned to Tyler and introduced him to his other guests. "This is Jackie, Kenneth, and Sammie."

"How are y'all doing?" Sammie said. "You can call me Sam."

The mayor said, "I invited them over for dinner to show my appreciation for what they did for my son. We just came from the table. Would you like something to eat?"

"Oh no, sir, I ate not long ago. Thanks anyway."

"If it wasn't for their compassion, my son wouldn't be here with us."

Tyler said, 'What do you mean?"

He said, "These fine young men took the time to stop and take my son, a stranger, to the hospital and that saved his life and I will be so ever grateful to them. Then they were arrested for something that they didn't do."

Tyler asked, "What did they say you did?"

Jackie said, "We were accused of beating someone to death the night we took Conner to the hospital. On that same night, another person was brought into the hospital ER, and he died. It was reported that we were the cause of his death. The police said that it was Conner who had died. Even though they didn't know his name, and we didn't know Conner's name."

"Man, that's awful," Tayler says. "Man, I would be highly p'ed off, angry, and mad.

Jackie said, "We were. It is tough to be accused of something that you know you didn't do. But as we look back on it, we feel that it was a test that God put before us. At the time, we weren't expecting a test from God, especially one of this magnitude.

"We were locked up, but we wouldn't give up. We prayed all night. We had to hold on to our faith because we knew that we were innocent, and on that same night, six or seven people—"

"Six," Kenneth interjected.

"—gave their life to God."

Kenneth said, "We had to learn that no matter what we are faced with, it is not about us. I believe that God allows some things to happen to build our faith and our character. We may not understand it, so we have to believe that God meant it for our good. We realize that it is not always clear what God wants us to do or how to go about doing it, we just have to trust in Him and He will work it out. We have been friends for a long time, and we have always had each other's back, even when we have done wrong to one another. Our love for each other is what helped us to stay together. If one of us does something against the other, we make sure we work it out and come to an agreement, and we don't hold it against each other.

"Look at us now. A bad situation has caused us to make new friends. Ain't God good?"

Tyler said, "You know, I can believe that. I met someone that I would have never taken the time out to talk too. He has become a good friend. There were some things that I was going through, and this guy just started talking to me. He is a homeless man. He talked to me about God. He changed my life."

Danny said, "Are you telling us that you found *God*?"

Tyler said, "Yes, I think I did."

Tyrone asked, "What happen to you? I thought the sky would have to fall in order for you to see the light."

"God wants us to get out of our comfort zone and stop judging each other and start helping each other," Sam said.

Tyrone said, "Man, I ain't judging, but I know this guy. And for him to say he found God, that is a big deal."

"Brother, you know me. I have been trying for years to get you to go to church with me. But you always tell me that you don't believe in that. Right now, I am so happy for you."

Conner spoke up and said as he was looking at Jackie, I remember when I asked you to take me to that hospital, and I remember getting in the van. I also remember you praying over me and I felt a peace come over me. I felt like I was in the present of God. I believe that God showed favor on me because of my father's faith. But I don't remember arriving to the hospital. Thank you for helping me.

"I know that my parents are God-fearing Christians, and they took me to church when I was younger. But when I got older, I strayed away. I heard of God, but I don't know Him. And I really need to get to know Him. No, I want to know Him. After all that I have been through, I have to make a change in my life. When I get a little better, I think that I will go find me a church to attend! I feel like it was God who was keeping me alive for some reason. I am sitting here, listening to you guys talk, and Jackie, you have this excitement in your voice when you talk about God. You sound happy and alive. That joy that you have—how can I get it? I bet, when you talk, people take note and listen to you."

Jackie said, "But it's not about me, it's the word that excites me. When you love the Lord, you should be excited. If you look back into the Old Testament and you read what the children of Israel had to do to atone their sins and what they had to sacrifice, and when you read about Jesus who came and sacrifice His life for our sins, one should be excited."

The mayor spoke up and said, to Jackie, but he was really talking to Conner, "You know, when I was growing up, my parents didn't take me to church, but I had this desire to go. On Sundays, I would ask my father if I could go visit a friend. On the way to his house, I would sneak in the back of a church just to hear what was going on. When the preacher was done preaching, I would run to my friend's house. I didn't want my father to find out that I was going to church. He didn't believe in God. I didn't want other people to know, and it got back to my father. I had a small Bible that I would read late at night when my parents were asleep. I would hide it between the mattresses in my room.

"One day, my mom found it and asked me about it. She didn't say anything to my father about it. Sometimes she and I would sit and read it when we knew that my father was not coming home soon. I said to myself when I was younger, that if I ever have children, I will take them to church so that they could hear the word, and I would never hold them back from doing what they want to do. I didn't want to be like my father. I love my son, and I tried to give him the best but at the same time teach him to love other no matter who they are or what their skin color. I tried to be a good father and set good examples."

"You are a good father," Conner said with tears rolling down his cheeks. "I am proud that you are my father! You taught me well. This is why I believe God saved me because He showed favor to you."

His father went over to Conner and hugged him real tight. "The first chance that I get, I am going to church and ask God to forgive me."

Sam said, "Do you know what the beauty of Jesus Christ is? You don't have to wait to go to church to repent of your sins and ask for forgiveness. You can do it wherever you are. You can give your life to God right now. If you believe that Jesus is the Son of God and He died on the cross and He rose from the dead, then you shall be saved. You must confess it with your mouth."

Tyrone said, "Man, I did it a long time ago and I'm glad that I did. When I was younger, I was headed down the wrong road. My mom told me, she said, 'Tyrone, the life that you are living is going to put you in the ground at a young age. I pray for you every day and night. I raised you right and I know you know better. You need to change so that I don't have to worry so much.' I was hurting my mother by what I was doing. So I changed and gave my life to Jesus. I may talk a lot of noise, but I know who my Jesus is."

Tyler said, "Man, why you never said anything to us about it?"

Tyrone said, "Man, like I said, I have been trying to talk to you, but you weren't ready to change. Everything was about you. God knew when you would be ready. So I stop pushing the issue."

Kenneth said, "That goes to show that we all have a pass. We all have done things and come short. But it was the grace and the goodness of God that kept us."

"And prayer!" the mayor said.

Tyler said to Kenneth, "I want to go to a good church this Sunday. Do you know where I could go and get good teaching?"

"Do you want to go to an all-white church?" Kenneth said.

Tyler got a little offended. "What do you mean by an all-white church?"

He said, "I didn't mean to offend you. It's just that people call themselves 'Christians,' and yet they only want to congregate with their own. That's black people and white."

"Why do you think that is?" Tyler said.

"Well, I think that they feel uncomfortable if they are not with their own race."

Tyler asked, "Do I seem uncomfortable around you? And do you feel uncomfortable in this white man's house?"

Kenneth said, "No."

"Then how can you make a judgement about someone feelings? Even though you might be right. But by you being a Christian, you should know not to make judgement or assumptions."

Kenneth said, "You are right, and I apologize to you. I did not mean to offend you. Please accept my apology."

Sam said to his friend, "Man, you sure put your foot in your mouth then."

Sam said to Tyler and the others, "Hey man, this Sunday we are having friends and family at the church, and we would like to invite you all as our new friends and special guest."

Tyler asked Kenneth jokingly, "Is this an all-white church?"

"You got me there. But, no, it's a diverse church," said Kenneth.

Sam said, "Can I count you all coming?"

The mayor says he would be honored to be there. Everyone said that they will be there as well. Tyler said he will be there but asked if he could bring a friend.

Sam said, "Sure, bring whoever you wish."

Conner asked Tyler who he planned to bring. He said, "I met someone in the park, and he has been teaching me about the Bible. I think that he would love to go."

Conner asked, "Do I know him?"

"No, he is very private. If he comes, I want him to meet you," said Tyler.

Tyrone said, "I will call the other fellows to see if they would like to go."

Jackie said, "Okay then, it's getting late, and we have to go. Thank you, mayor, for inviting us over. Conner, we are glad to see you doing better."

Tyler, Tyrone, and Danny said, "We better be going too. Thanks for everything."

So they all went out the door to go their separate ways. Tyler turned back and hugged Conner and said, "I love you, man."

Conner said, "I know, and don't worry, all is forgiven. Tyler turned and left feeling that Conner has forgiven him.

The next time Tyler met up with Kelvin, he told him about the invitation to the church and told him that he will go if he would go with him. Kelvin saw on Tyler's face what it meant to him, and he said yes. Kelvin felt that it was time for him to go back to church with a different prospective and without fear of rejection.

Chapter 24

S unday morning at Mt. Olive Grove Baptist Church, the church was packed to its maximum. They had chairs in the aisles and in the foyer. There were people who had never been to this church before just showing up. Some were invited, and some just came on their own.

Jackie, Kenneth, and Sam were standing at the entryway, looking and waiting for the guests they invited. Finally, the mayor and his family arrived. Tyrone and Danny had invited a few other friends as well. Tyler was still waiting in the parking lot, looking and hoping that Kelvin would show up. He was very nervous. He was standing near his car, pacing and talking to himself.

Is he going to come? I should have went and picked him up. A few minutes later, he said to himself, *Okay, he is not coming. I'm going in.*

By the time he started to go inside, he heard someone call his name. "Hey, Tyler."

He turned and saw Kelvin coming across the parking lot. With a big smile on his face, he said, "Man, I thought that you weren't going to make it."

Kelvin said, "I had a little trouble this morning, but I didn't want to let you down. I have disappointed too many people in my life and I have changed. So I have to start keeping my word. Okay, let's go in."

When they walked in to the church, Kenneth had his back turned to the door as Tyler and Kelvin walked in. Tyler introduced Kelvin to Jackie, Sam, and Kenneth at the same time. Kenneth turned around, but they didn't recognize him.

Kelvin said to them, "You don't remember me?"

Sam said, "Have we met somewhere before?"

He said, "I'm Kelvin. We met in jail and you helped me turn my life around."

Kenneth looked at him hard and said, "*Kelvin*! Is that you? *Oh my God*, it is you." Kenneth grabbed Kelvin and hugged him with great love. He was so excited to see Kelvin. He thought that he would never see him again. After he got over the excited greeting, Kenneth asked Kelvin if he would do a song. He remembered him singing in the jail and how beautiful he sounded.

Kelvin said, "I didn't come to be a part of this program."

Kenneth said, "I know but will you?"

He agreed to do it.

Kelvin's mother and father were there, but they didn't know he was there, and he didn't know that they were there as well. Kelvin and Tyler took a seat on the far side of the church, opposite to his parents.

When the praise team and the pastor came out to start the service, they were very surprised to see the church so full. They began to sing songs of praises, and the congregation was praising, singing, and shouting along with the praise team. The people came to receive the Lord. There was so many people crying and praying. It seemed like they had been hurting and searching for a long time. They needed God to free them from their bondage, from their stronghold—they wanted to be delivered. Some were thanking God for delivering them from their bondage.

It seemed as if no one cared what someone thought of them at the time, all they wanted was to hear from God. The spirit was in this place. There were so many people that were moved by the Holy Spirit, the saved and the unsaved were crying. Some looked confused, and some looked lost. However, they were overjoyed.

After the praise and worship service was over and everything had settled down, the mistress of ceremony called on Ms. Jaleel Waters to do a reading. She came up and did her protocol, addressing everyone. She said, "The title of my reading is, 'Are You a Hoarder?'"

People started looking around and at each other. They were wondering where she was going to go with that.

She started:

"When we think about hoarders, we think about people who collect junk that is of no value and store it in and around their home. Everywhere you look, all you see is junk. They have so much junk, they can barely move around in their home or yard. In their home, they have a path that they can barely walk through. Wall to wall junk. The house smells bad. Dead rodents. Roaches crawling. Filthy sinks, bathrooms and the floors. The house is just filthy, and it's unfit to live in. The house is so junky, it can make you sick on the stomach. The majority of hoarders live alone, and they are passionate about what they have collected. They have no friends. Their family members are ashamed of them and they don't come around to visit. No one comes to visit, and they are lonely people.

"When you see a hoarder, you talk bad about them and you wonder, 'How can they live like that with all that junk?' They should be ashamed. You frown with disgust on your face. Hoarders hold on tight to their junk. They know that they have to get rid of that junk, but they have been holding on to so much junk for so long that they can't let it go. When someone tries to help them clean up, they are all in until the process begins. When it's time to clean, they want to pick and choose what goes and what stays. They end up keeping more than what they let go, and they haven't made any improvement.

"I have a question for you. Are you a hoarder? You might say, 'Who me? I know that I'm no hoarder, my house is clean.' Is your house really clean? What kind of junk are you holding on to that is keeping God from entering into your home—your heart? How do you know if you are a hoarder? Has someone hurt you or broke your heart in the past and you can't find it in your heart to forgive them? Has someone disappointed you and you are still holding it against them? Do you have envy? Are you holding onto hatred toward someone? Are you jealous? Are you backstabbing someone because you don't like them? If someone you had a misunderstanding with comes to you and asks for forgiveness, you say, 'Okay, I forgive you,' but you still talk about that person when they are not around and you avoid that person because you are still holding on to your anger.

"Are you a hoarder? When you walk around mad at the world because you can't have your way, and someone says the wrong thing to you and your feelings are hurt, are you hoarding? When you are hoarding, you think that it's all about you, and it's not. Holding on to junk makes you sick. When you are holding onto junk, you have no joy. You look sad. You're tired all the time. That junk is weight that's holding you down. How can God dwell in you with all that junk? He can't enter into your heart, and if He does, He can't move around.

"It is my understanding that God doesn't dwell in unclean places, but He can make the unclean clean. So if you are hoarding, how can He dwell in you? He is standing at the door, knocking, but you can't let him in because you have so much junk in your house. You can't get to the door to open it. If only you realize that if you open the door—your heart—and let Him in, He will help you clean that junk out of your house.

"Ephesians 4:31–32 says,

> Let all bitterness, and wrath, and anger, and clamor, and evil speaking, be put away from you, with all malice. And be ye kind to one another, tenderhearted, forgiving one another, even as God for Christ's sake hath forgiven you.

"As Christians, we should not allow ourselves to become hoarders of junk. Instead we should be disciples for Christ. Show love and the joy of Christ, not just to another Christian, but to non-Christians as well. God created all of us. So how can we say bad things about His creation? We all have some good in us."

After she was done reading, the people started talking in a low voice about her reading. For some, it touched home and they felt convicted. Kelvin's mother and father were whispering to each other about how they feel about their son. His mother began to cry. Her heart was heavy. She felt guilty about how she treated her son when he came to her home.

After a couple more readings and a song, the pastor got up to preach his sermon. He says in a deep rugged voice, "If you have your Bibles, I want you to go with me to Luke chapter 15, and we are going to start reading from the verse 11." He read from verse 11 through 32.

He said, "My subject is 'Forgiveness is not as hard as you make it.' Why is it that people hang on to anger, hurt, and the thought of being betrayed? Is it that you want the person that you are angry with to feel your pain? You want them to hurt just as much as you are hurting. Even though you love the person, you don't want them to forget what they did to you. When you are having those kinds of emotions, all you are doing is making the situation about you.

"Is it really about how you feel? When you are disappointed in someone, you feel betrayed. Instead of you trying to find out why this person is doing what he is doing, you try to analyze the problem yourself and talk about it to someone who has nothing to do with the situation. You talk to everybody that you can get to listen to you about the situation but not the source.

"The person that caused you to feel the way that you do comes to you for forgiveness, but you shunt them away. You are so angry with him, you can't see what God is trying to do in your life. Forgiveness is not as hard as you make it.

"As we look at the story about the prodigal son, I ask myself—is this story about the son or about the father? I think that is more so about the father.

"This father had two sons. We don't know the age difference, but I can imagine that they had a few years between them. I can imagine the father was a hard man, a God-fearing man, and tough on his sons. The young son felt like he wasn't loved by his father because of the way his father raised him. The young son didn't want to follow his father's strict rules. He was tired of working hard every day, not being appreciated and not having fun. So he went to his father and asked for his portion of his inheritance.

"When he received his portion, I can imagine that he was talking to his older brother, 'Man, I'm getting out of here. Man, pop is too hard on us and he is old-fashioned. I want to enjoy myself before I get too old.' I can imagine that his older brother was trying to talk some sense into him. But he wouldn't listen. I can see his father in his room praying to God to protect his son while he is out in the wilderness.

"A few days later, the son took off with all the belongings that he could carry. He got far away from his father as he could. He had money in his pocket, and he was feeling good. He made friends fast. The women were at his beckoning call—one on both arms. He bought everybody a round of drinks. He felt like he was the man, and everybody loved him. He partied night after night, and he was having a good time. At the time, he wasn't thinking about putting some money to the side in case he needed something to fall back on. The Bible says that he squandered his property in reckless living. When he didn't have any more money, a great famine arose in that country, and he began to be in need.

"When he had money, he had friends. Now that he has no money, he has no friends. Look how God works. The famine was not in every country, only in the country that the young man was in. He was broke and hungry. I believe that he was too prideful and ashamed to go back to his father. So he went out seeking a job so that he could get enough money to feed himself. The only job that he could get was to feed the pigs. By this time hunger was so bad, he began to eat the pods that the pigs were eating. The Bible says that no one gave him anything.

"I believe that the father had heard that there was a famine going on in that country where his son was. While his son was going through hard times, I believe that his father was still praying for his son. I believe that God heard his prayer and caused his son to come to his senses.

"The Bible says, 'But when he came to himself, he said, "How many of my father's hired servants have more than enough bread, but I perish here with hunger! I will arise and go to my father, and I will say to him, 'Father, I have sinned against heaven and before you. I am no longer worthy to be called your son. Treat me as one of your hired servants.'" And he arose and came to his father.'

"I can see the father standing on his front porch, looking across the fields. 'But while he was still a long way off, his father saw him and felt compassion, and ran and embraced him and kissed him. And the son said to him, "Father, I have sinned against heaven and before you. I am no longer worthy to be called your son."

"His father didn't hold any anger. He didn't say, 'I told you so. He didn't criticize him for being rebellious. He welcomed him home as if he had been away to college or in the army. He gave him a hero's welcome home. The father knew what his son had done, but he wanted his son to know that he loves him so much and all is forgiven. His son was home and alive. That was important to the father."

As the pastor was speaking, Kelvin's mother was sitting there with her head down, weeping and sobbing for her son. Her husband was crying as well as he was trying to comfort his wife. She felt like she missed the opportunity to welcome her son back home when he came to visit her. She remembered that she closed the door in his face. Now as this pastor was speaking about the prodigal son, she had regrets. She felt like there was no one else in the room, and the pastor was talking directly to her.

"I may never see my son again," she said to her husband.

He told her, "When the service is over, we will go look for him. I miss him too."

The pastor was still in his sermon. He said, "The Bible tells us that the father told his servant, 'Go quickly and bring me a robe and put it on him, put the ring on his finger and sandals on his feet. And bring the fattened calf and kill it, and let us eat and celebrate. For this my son was dead, and is alive again; he was lost, and is found.' And they began to celebrate.

"Forgiveness is not as hard as you make it." He said, "You can't celebrate the goodness of God if you can't forgive. Asking someone for forgiveness is for you to start the process of healing."

Forgiveness is strong medicine.

I can see that when his son returned home, he didn't have to have an explanation for his return. The father was happy to have his son home alive and well. However the son felt the need for forgiveness from his father and God. The son didn't just walked out on his father, he tried to walk out on God. Even though the son wanted to live in sin, God still loved him. God allowed him to do all that he though he wanted to do. God showed him that a life of sin will lead to destruction. When God has had enough of your sin, he will put you in a place where you don't want to be.

As the pastor was speaking those words, Kelvin was thinking about his lowest point and how God delivered him. Tyler was thinking about when he was about to end his life and God sent Kelvin to intercede. You can tell by the look on the congregations faces that they were remembering a low point in their lives, when God sent an angel their way. Some were whispering to each other.

The pastor said, remember the children of Israel, when they rebelled against God, He removed them from the land He promised them into exile. He cause them to suffer under the hands of a foreign King. But, He loved them and brought them back home. When you ask God for forgiveness and repent of your sins, He can restore you better than you were before.

As the pastor was ending his sermon, someone gave him a note that read, "we have a special guest to sing a song before you close out."

He said, the doors of the church are open. If you have not given your souls to God, now is a good time to get your life right with God. About ten to fifteen people came before the Alter to be saved by Jesus Christ. There were other ministers that gathered around them and prayed with them. They were escorted to a back room in the church.

The pastor made the announcement that before we dismissed, we had a special request for a song by Mr. Calvin. The person that gave the pastor the note misspelled Kelvin's name. Kelvin's mother heard the name Calvin, so she didn't pay that close attention to the person. She was in her own world asking God to give her another chance to make it right with her son. Give her another opportunity to hold her child in her arms. She had her head down as Kelvin walked to the front of the church.

Kelvin starts to sing and his voice was smooth and easy to listen too. His mom begin to cry even more. She looks up at her husband

and said, he sounds like my baby used to sound, so she kept on listing. In Kelvin's song there is a high note that he used to reach when he was in his mom church choir. When he reached that note, the church erupted. His mom shouted at the top of her voice. THAT'S MY BABY!!!!!!! KELVIN!!!!! KELVIN!!!!! KELVIN!!!!!! As she was calling his name, she was trying to make her way to him. Everyone was looking and wandering what was going on, but she didn't care. As she was crying and screaming her baby's name, Kelvin was looking to see who was calling his name. He moved to the center aisle to see who was calling his name. When he saw that it was his mother, he yelled, MAMMA!!!! MAMMA!!! Mamma!!! As he was making his way to her he said, I'm sorry momma!!!! I'm sorry momma!!! Momma I love you. I'm so sorry mamma. They meet in the middle of the aisles and hugged each other so tight. They were crying and asking each other for forgiveness. They both were saying that they were sorry for hurting each other. "Forgive me mamma, please forgive me! Whatever you want me to do, I will do it. I love you mamma!! Whatever you want me to do, I will do it. I just want you to love me again. Mamma please forgive me. I missed you mamma. Just love me mamma!!" She says with a soft voice, "No, baby I never stop loving you."

She said "forgive me Kelvin", I should have had more compassion and understanding. I should have been there when you needed me the most. "No, mamma it was my fault, I don't blame you, you tried to tell me but I wouldn't listen." They kelp embracing each other and crying. He tried to explain to his mamma, but she stopped him. "No, baby no need to explain; you are here now. That's all that matters."

By that time his father came up and joined in the hugging. He put his arms around both of them. All three of them standing in the middle of the isles embraced and cried, the congregation was in tears as well. Kelvin looked at his father and said, "please forgive me father." He said, "I do" and asked his son to forgive him too. We all need forgiveness.

At the same time Tyler asked Conner why did he forgave him for what he did. Conner said, "you and I have been best of friends for most of our lives. I couldn't throw that a way because of this one mistake. I know that if I had not been irritating you and knowing that you were upset, you would have took care of me. I know that you love me and I love you. You are my best friend and my brother. I know you and if the tables were turned, you would forgive me. It was not easy to forgive at first, but when you came to my bed side at the hospital, I heard what you were saying and the sincerity in your voice, I knew you meant what you were saying. So, I had too, for you and me."

The pastor tried to compose himself as he was dealing with his own personal issues. He was crying because his daughter had left home and hadn't spoken to him in three years. The pastor said to himself, "I must be the one to reach out for peace with my daughter today."

He stood up with his eyes red, tears rolling down his face and said to the congregation, if you have someone who needs forgiving, seek them out as soon as possible. You are dismissed.

And the church said AMEN.

My Mother's Prayer

Dear Lord

Grant me wisdom and knowledge and understanding of your word. Use me in a way that you want to use me. Guide my footsteps through a safe path and let your angles cover me as I go through the days of my life. Show me how to walk in your footsteps so that I can live a healthy and prosperous life. Lord I ask this in Jesus name. Amen, Amen and amen. Thank you, Jesus.

Elsie W. Frazier

About the Author

M r. Nathan was born in southeast Georgia. He was raised by a single mother along with two sisters. He is married to his lovely wife Maggie, he has a daughter and a son, Alesia, and Malcolm. Mr. Nathan started writing short stories about five years ago. God would give him a word for a day, and he would write a short inspirational story on that word.

The community churches would come together and have a singing festival, and he would take the title of each song and make a story from the songs that were sung. He believes God was preparing him for this book. He struggled with forgiving someone, and God kept dealing with him to get it right.

This book started out as a dream and God told him to write it down. The more God poured on him, the more he wrote. He would write whenever he would get a chance.

He never thought that he would write a book, but he realized that it's not what he thinks; it's God's will.

CPSIA information can be obtained
at www.ICGtesting.com .
Printed in the USA
LVHW091158131020
668666LV00007B/798